The JESUS We FORGOT

Knowing the God of the Word and not just the Word of God

Brent Shores

WESTBOW
PRESS
A DIVISION OF THOMAS NELSON
& ZONDERVAN

Copyright © 2019 Brent Shores.

All rights reserved. No part of this book may be used or reproduced by any means, graphic, electronic, or mechanical, including photocopying, recording, taping or by any information storage retrieval system without the written permission of the author except in the case of brief quotations embodied in critical articles and reviews.

This book is a work of non-fiction. Unless otherwise noted, the author and the publisher make no explicit guarantees as to the accuracy of the information contained in this book and in some cases, names of people and places have been altered to protect their privacy.

Unless otherwise indicated, scripture quotations are taken from the New American Standard Bible® (NASB), Copyright © 1960, 1962, 1963, 1968, 1971, 1972, 1973, 1975, 1977, 1995 by The Lockman Foundation. Used by permission. www.lockman.org

Scripture taken from the King James Version of the Bible.

WestBow Press books may be ordered through booksellers or by contacting:

WestBow Press
A Division of Thomas Nelson & Zondervan
1663 Liberty Drive
Bloomington, IN 47403
www.westbowpress.com
1 (866) 928-1240

Because of the dynamic nature of the Internet, any web addresses or links contained in this book may have changed since publication and may no longer be valid. The views expressed in this work are solely those of the author and do not necessarily reflect the views of the publisher, and the publisher hereby disclaims any responsibility for them.

Any people depicted in stock imagery provided by Getty Images are models, and such images are being used for illustrative purposes only.
Certain stock imagery © Getty Images.

ISBN: 978-1-9736-5044-7 (sc)
ISBN: 978-1-9736-5045-4 (hc)
ISBN: 978-1-9736-5043-0 (e)

Library of Congress Control Number: 2019900187

Print information available on the last page.

WestBow Press rev. date: 02/06/2019

Contents

Introduction vii

Part 1 — The Treasure 1

Treasure in the Field 2
The Word Of God 18
Knowing God 34
Kingdom Come 55
My Yoke is Easy 73

Part 2 — The Foundations 83

Grace To Live 84
Faith is a Substance 102
Be Holy 112
The Spirit 123
Growing 160

Part 3 - The Path 175

The Beginning of Wisdom 176
The Greatest Command 189
Wait on the Lord 223
Testing of Faith 240
Conclusion 255

About the Author 257

Introduction

The goal of this book is not a call to missions.
　It's not a call to giving.
　It's not a call to service.
　It's not a call to ministry.
　It's not a call to fasting.
　It's not even a call to prayer.
　It's a call for the church to come back to its God.
　That might sound odd, but history has a way of repeating itself.
　Israel stood before their tents in front of Mount Sinai as God Himself came down upon the mountain in thunder, lightning, and fire. Imagine, the Israelites seeing the glory of God manifest upon the earth. They had been called out by the Almighty God to be His own people.
　Their response:

> And when the people saw it, they trembled and stood at a distance. Then they said to Moses, "Speak to us yourself and we will listen; but let not God speak to us, or we will die." – Exodus 20:18-19

　They pulled away. Rather than chancing an encounter with a true and living God, they chose to follow Moses. Let Moses take the risk; let Moses spend the time — they just wanted to live their lives.
　Today, God is still moving. His glory still appears and He can still be found by those who are hungry enough. The church stands at the door and watches. Will they choose to stand before God, being a nation of priests and kings as He wished, or will they safely stay behind their pastors and ministers? Will they come to know the Living God themselves, or stick with their Bibles and their commentaries that let them live more comfortably?
　Can I show you how to do this? Not exactly. I suspect everyone's

path is a little different. Besides, I'm more like a dog who has the scent. I have glimpses and find Him here and there, but don't walk in what I know is available yet. What I can do is point you in the direction. I can remind you of this God who called you, and who is still waiting to walk with you. Let's speak of the Jesus we have forgotten.

PART 1 — THE TREASURE

The kingdom of heaven is like a treasure hidden in the field, which a man found and hid again; and from joy over it he goes and sells all that he has and buys that field.

—Matthew 13:44

Treasure in the Field

Why Did Jesus Come?

The truth we know can sometimes be our greatest crutch. The beliefs that we've held can block us from finding a better way or a deeper truth. Haven't we all seen people following useless actions because that is how they have always done it? I wonder at their ability to not question why. Now I want to ask you, do you have the humility to take an honest look at what you know? If not, then perhaps this isn't the book for you. If you know the answers already, then I won't have much for you—and unfortunately, neither will God. Yet, if you are willing to question yourself at times, then you still have room to grow, for the Christian life is filled with moments of humility.

Tell me—what would you say was the reason that Jesus came to earth? The obvious answer, which was the reason I "knew," was to save us from hell. He came to die and forgive us for our sins. By His death we can now find salvation, and when we die we go to heaven. Some variation of this would be the default answer for most who have been in church. Having cleared that up, let's take a look at Jesus's last prayer with His disciples before He went to the cross. Being His last, you would expect Him to lift up those things that were most important to Him and the things that His disciples needed to hear.

> Jesus spoke these things; and lifting up His eyes to heaven, He said, "Father, the hour has come; glorify Your Son, that the Son may glorify You, even as You gave Him authority over all flesh, that to all whom You have given Him, He may give eternal life." — (John 17:1–2)

Jesus's first thought was to glorify God. Jesus was here for His glory, and to lift Him up. After this, we find that Jesus said He came to give eternal life to those who follow God. There we are—our answer. Most of us can quote this next verse.

> For God so loved the world that he gave his one and only Son, that whoever believes in him shall not perish but have eternal life. — (John 3:16)

Fire Insurance

Throughout my life, I had always felt we had something a little off here. We teach eternal life as living in heaven with God after we die. We preach repentance with concepts like "fire protection," "you can't pull a trailer when you die," "not fearing death," and "assurance of heaven." Don't get me wrong. I'm not saying that these things are wrong, but they do seem to captivate too much of our attention. Have you ever had trouble convincing someone why he or she should become a Christian when you can only provide for the future and not now?

It's like life insurance. Honestly, I would make a horrible salesman for life insurance. I feel like I would have to feed off the fears of someone dying to make a living. There are better ways to come at this, and I have a good friend who does sell insurance and does a great job. I fear that I would get stuck on the dying part and not focus upon the good it can do. Guess I'm just not up to the challenge. In the same way, this is how I sometimes felt about witnessing to someone. Let me scare you to make you fear death in order to bring you to God. If you were to die, this is how you can protect yourself. That's good news, but is it "the good news"? That's what the word *gospel* means: the good news. In fact, I once heard a minister say that the actual translation of the word used for the gospel comes out to something more like "the almost too good to be true news."

Instead we treat life like a game we might play. Eternal life is our finish line, and we need to accumulate enough points to make it there before our time runs out. Life may be hard, unfair, and taxing, but at the end of this game is all the happiness in the world. All we need to do is just hold out until we get there. We may not come out and say this, but if you watch our messages and how we comfort others, this is what you often find. Unfortunately, this sells the gospel short.

What Is Eternal Life?

Let's take a step back to that passage from John 17. In verse 2 we find that to every person who received Jesus, God gave them "eternal life." It's easy to glaze over this and believe we know that eternal life means going to heaven. We mistakenly take the literal translation that eternal life is a life that never ends. In some translations of the Bible, you will even find it translated as "everlasting life." Now is when I ask you to broaden your view. Perhaps it is more than what we give it credit for. This is something that took me fifteen years as a Christian to finally catch. All I had to do was move one more verse on without my preconceptions.

> Now this is eternal life: that they may know you, the only true God, and Jesus Christ, whom you have sent. — (John 17:3)

Jesus's definition of eternal life was not going to heaven when we die. Nor was it living forever. Instead, His definition was to know God and His Son, Jesus—nothing more and nothing less. Imagine that. We often preach that salvation is coming back to God so that we may go to heaven; yet I don't believe that was Jesus's primary goal. One of them, for sure, since it's all caught up together, but perhaps not the primary one. Jesus came that we might know God. I want to be very clear on this next point. This is not that we come to know Him when we reach heaven, but that we may know Him *now*. We can have an intimate relationship with Him *now*. Eternal life begins *now* and not at our physical death.

Consider Adam and Eve—what were they created for? There were no lost to save, no homeless to feed, and no missions to take on.

They were given the earth to watch over, and in the evenings, God would come walk with them in the garden. They didn't have things to ask God for, just conversation to make. Adam and Eve were created to rule this world and to fellowship with God. This intimacy with God was lost when Adam and Eve sinned. Fortunately, Jesus died to restore us back to our lost position with God. Here's the point I'm trying to get across that I hope you don't miss. The primary reason for Jesus's death was not to bring us to heaven, but to bring us back into relationship. Humankind wasn't created as a servant, but as a friend.

> And we know that the Son of God has come, and has given us understanding so that we may know Him who is true; and we are in Him who is true, in His Son Jesus Christ. This is the true God and eternal life. — (1 John 5:20)

True life comes from knowing God. If we truly know Jesus, we will believe and be saved. If we know God, our lives will forever be altered. When we come to know God, everything changes. We find that this world we live in has a new depth to it. We find God moving among it all and love flowing through all things. The ability to live forever in heaven is an outflow of the life that comes from knowing God. Let us throw away our ideologies, our preconceived notions, and our experiential understandings. We tend to clutter the truth with our understanding anyway. Instead, let's start building again upon the Word. God made us to have a relationship with Him. That's where we begin.

New Covenant

Even in the Old Testament we find this to be true. The old covenant was filled with laws and separation, but Jeremiah prophesied a new covenant for us.

> "Behold, days are coming," declares the Lord, "when I will make a new covenant with the house of Israel and with the house of Judah, not like the covenant which I made with their fathers in the day I took them by the hand to bring them out of the land of Egypt, My covenant which they broke, although I was a husband to them," declares the Lord. "But this is the covenant which I will make with the house of Israel after those days," declares the Lord, "I will put My law within them and on their heart I will write it; and I will be their God, and they shall be My people. They will not teach again, each man his neighbor and each man his brother, saying 'Know the Lord,' for they will all know Me, from the least of them to the greatest of them," declares the Lord, "for I will forgive their iniquity, and their sin I will remember no more." – (Jeremiah 31:31–34)

In this new covenant, God will teach us His law Himself. He will write it upon our hearts, and not on tablets of stone. Most amazingly, we shall be God's people and we shall know Him. The Lord clearly states that each person can know Him. Jesus came for this purpose. Continuing to the next verse after John 3:16, we find this:

> For God did not send his Son into the world to condemn the world, but to save the world through him. — (John 3:17)

He didn't come to condemn us as some of our fellow Christians do. They prefer to preach a message of condemnation over everyone: preaching fear, sin, and judgement. That is not why Jesus was here. He would, of course, correct when it was necessary—especially among the self-righteous Pharisees. However, God did not send Him here for this reason. He sent Him here to save us and to bring us eternal life. Jesus was sent to bring much more than just salvation to us.

Life More Abundant

> The thief comes only to steal and kill and destroy; I came that they may have life, and have it abundantly. — (John 10:10)

The devil comes to take things away. He is happy for us to live our lives in fear rather than relationship, because it keeps us in line. He wants God's blessings for us, our success, and our very lives. When you see the types of evil in the world—the killings, the thefts, and the sicknesses—remember that God did not bring them. We did. God gave authority over this world to humans, and we passed that along to the devil. This allowed all these things to come upon the world. In contrast, Jesus came to bring us an abundant life. We aren't meant to just survive this time upon earth, but to live it well. Our life is a testament to God's goodness. What is this sort of life that Jesus is giving unto us? Let's look at His comments to the Samaritan woman He met at the well.

> If you knew the gift of God, and who it is who says to you, "Give Me a drink," you would have asked Him, and He would have given you living water…
>
> Everyone who drinks of this water will thirst again; but whoever drinks of the water that I will give him shall never thirst; but the water that I will give him will become in him a well of water springing up to eternal life. — (John 4:10,13–14)

Again, I find it easy to skim over verses which I have so often read. As soon as I read about the water causing us to not thirst, I immediately replace this with salvation and move on to the next verse. In doing so, I miss part of the point. I can't just take *thirst*, apply salvation, and move on. Jesus told this woman that when she drank of the water He gave, she would never thirst again. Thirst is a sensation that God has given us as an indication of a need we have. In situations like this, I've often found that Jesus was more concerned for the heart of the person than their body. Given the context of the conversation, we can assume He wasn't speaking of physical water. This indicates He was giving out water for the soul and spirit. If that is the case, then I must admit I still find myself thirsty. I often find myself longing for things in my life to have more meaning. I long for something that will bring satisfaction to my heart.

> These things I have spoken to you so that My joy may be in you, and that your joy may be made full. — (John 15:11)

Do you find yourself full of joy? Joy is one of the fruits of the spirit that is obvious when you are lacking it. In the list of the fruits of the spirit it comes in second, right after love. Joy should be an obvious indication that we know God. If we know Him, we will have joy. How can we not find joy in the knowledge that the God of the universe has sought after us? That He will watch over us? Paul said it very simply to the Thessalonians.

> Rejoice always. — (1 Thessalonians 5:16)

I've heard it said, "if you're not happy on this earth, don't come up to heaven and ruin it for the rest of us." The speaker said this with a bit of humor, yet there is also truth in it. As a follower of Christ, I have purpose, hope, and security. What more could I ask for? I have a God who has sought me out and sacrificed His Son to get me back. He created such beauty around me for my pleasure. I have found that the closer I get to God, the more I laugh and smile. Our world is filled with wonders. If you don't find your life full of joy, perhaps you should take that as an opportunity to come before God and ask why.

Is There A Trick?

The hard part is drawing closer to Him. I remember a specific day as I was talking to God on the way to my car after leaving work. To give you a little context—let me say that I enjoy reading and hearing about fellow believers who see more of the kingdom. By that, I mean they see the kingdom manifested in this world. Stories like the disciples who healed the sick, received heavenly visitations, saw miracles, and spoke face to face with the Lord. I desire for our God to be more real in my life. I want a faith that can bring the spiritual into the physical. For this reason, as I was walking, I was pondering on some of these stories and asked God, "What's the trick to get this?"

First off, I hope some of you shuddered when you read my question to the Lord. You may not know exactly why, but hopefully you felt that something wasn't right there. What I was really saying to the Lord is, "what things do I have to do to get you to give me these experiences?" In other words, what are the steps to get my prayers answered? If you find yourself looking for a formula to make it happen, be wary. There is no formula to relationship. Ask any married couple. There are laws and truths, but God is not a computer to be programmed. Have you not often heard people give criteria on how to have your prayers answered? Why it is that God answers some requests and not others? In this particular experience, there was so much God could've said and so many ways He could've responded to me. Luckily, He's a gracious God, and He chose to correct me very gently. I heard this soft reply in my heart, "is there a trick to my love?"

Now let me ask you a question. Are you more interested in the benefits of God or the relationship with Him? There is a place we can reach with God when other things stop mattering. At that point, you don't need to make a difference, be a leader, see people healed, or be well known. You just need to be with God. When the primary focus of your heart is to love Him; all these other things will overflow out of that. When you get there, you will find that you're so in love with Him you can't help but share. For you can't keep from introducing others to your beloved.

One Thing

We can know God.

Sometimes I must stop and remind myself of this, because the truth of it is so amazing. What more do you need? David found this truth. He saw how important it was to know Him and to have that time with Him. Let me show you a section from one of his psalms.

> One thing I ask from the Lord, this only do I seek: that I may dwell in the house of the Lord all the days of my life, to gaze on the beauty of the Lord and to seek him in his temple. — (Psalm 27:4)

This was from the well-known 27th Psalm where David asks, *"whom shall I fear?"* He first spoke of what the Lord was to him; then he spoke about being surrounded by enemies but not afraid. After all this, David tells us the one thing he desires. The one thing he's asking of God. Though surrounded by enemies, his most important request was to be near God. David sought after dwelling in God's house, beholding His beauty, and spending time meditating upon Him in His temple.

What do you seek? Do you seek your own pleasures and recognition, or do you seek God? Is the one thing that drives you knowing more of Him? If not, then let me say that you might want to reassess your priorities. Jesus told Martha in that iconic scene with her sister Mary, "only one thing is necessary" (Luke 10:42). Eternal life boils down to knowing God. Make that your priority. Make that the "one thing" that leads you above all else. A successful Christian life comes as an outflow from being near to God. To know God, you must be with Him. When Moses led the Israelites out of Egypt, God gave him a choice. The Israelites had just turned from God. They had created a golden calf to worship even after all the amazing things the Lord had done bringing them out of Egypt. The Lord was very angry with them, and Moses interceded to save them from His wrath. After the Lord chose to spare them, He spoke these words concerning the Israelites.

> I will send an angel before you and I will drive out the Canaanite, the Amorite, the Hittite, the Perizzite, the Hivite and the Jebusite. Go up to a land flowing with milk and honey; for I will not go up in your midst, because you are an obstinate people, and I might destroy you on the way. — (Exodus 33:2–3)

God had decided to stay His hand and was ready to send them on; however, He would not accompany them. After nearly being destroyed by an angry God, that would probably sound like a reasonable deal to the Israelites. God would pave the way for them to the promised land. Moses didn't agree.

> Then he said to Him, "If Your presence does not go with us, do not lead us up from here. For how then can it be known that I have found favor in Your sight, I and Your people? Is it not by Your going with us, so that we, I and Your people, may be distinguished from all the other people who are upon the face of the earth?" — (Exodus 33:15–16)

If you don't come, then don't send us on. Moses understood, the power is in the presence. We are only a light to the world when the light is inside us. The conscious awareness of God's presence in our lives changes how we react to the world around us. Only when we let our awareness of our problems exceed our awareness of God do we fall to sin. When we come to find our hope in God's presence, then we can make a difference to those around us.

Our Portion

> Then the Lord said to Aaron, "You shall have no inheritance in their land nor own any portion among them; I am your portion and your inheritance among the sons of Israel." — (Numbers 18:20)

Once Israel reached the promised land, the Lord divided the land as an inheritance among the tribes of Israel. Each tribe received a portion to live on except for the tribe of Levi. God had set them aside to serve only as ministers. From them, He required more. They were to be His priests, and as His priests they were to live only off His provision. The Levites were not given any portion of land to sustain them. Instead, for example, they would feed themselves from a portion of the sacrifices that were made to God. Their reliance upon the Lord made them acceptable to serve before Him. David understood that this was more than just a rule for the Levites.

> The Lord is my portion; I have promised to keep Your words. — (Psalm 119:57)

Under the new covenant God desires that we may all be priests before Him. Accepting the Lord as our portion means that we set aside our possessions and expectations so that we may set our hearts upon the Lord and upon what He has set aside for us. We must realize that the Lord is more important, to be relied upon above all else. Though many Christians say this, we still rely upon our jobs, our health, and our families. That is why we see people become so desperate when they lose something. They've come to rely too heavily upon their income, and find they don't know how to trust in the Lord to care for them. He's been doing it all along, why would He stop? In my life, I've found that when I have problems at work, issues with my possessions, or even friction in my family; the closer I am walking with the Lord, the less it worries me. Why is this? It is because I have begun to make the Lord my portion. I am slowly changing what I hold onto in life and setting the worth of my life upon the Lord. In Him I find hope, love, and worth. Why should I allow the world to affect me, when my worth is found in Him? When we set our focus correctly, we'll find contentment with our lot.

> I am not saying this because I am in need, for I have learned to be content whatever the circumstances. I know what it is to be in need, and I know what it is to have plenty. I have learned the secret of being content in any and every situation, whether well fed or hungry, whether living in plenty or in want. I can do all this through him who gives me strength. — (Philippians 4:11–13)

Paul found his contentment in the Lord. This allowed him to suffer through innumerable troubles and still be found praising the Lord in prison or ministering to people after being stoned. We are to rely upon the Lord and not the things He's given us. We keep our hearts upon Him, treasuring Him and not His gifts.

What Is Your Treasure

Thinking back upon many of the stories in the Old Testament, I realized that I would often read about Israel and look down upon them. I saw them grumbling in the desert each day as God provided manna from heaven. I saw them doubting God's power to save them after all the plagues had struck Egypt. Most especially, I saw them turning to idols while Moses was up on the mountain meeting God. This was a reoccurring theme with them. Over and over God would move, and then they would drift back to their old ways. I often wondered why God would choose a people so apt to stray from Him; all the time not realizing how condescending my attitude was. I believed myself to be better than they, but I'm not. You see, my idols are not of gold and silver as so many of theirs were. My idols are my job, my family, my money and my entertainment. Idolatry is nothing more than putting another treasure in the place of God. After I came to realize this, I began to listen to contestants in talent competitions on television speak of how this competition is "everything to them." Rather than being proud, I fear for our culture as we praise them for their devotion. Is it devotion or idolatry?

Now take a minute to think about your passions. What are you passionate about in your life? What is it that you dream of during the day? When you go to bed, what thoughts cross your mind as you drop off into sleep? When you awake, what motivates you to get up? Do you look forward to your next paycheck, the new episode of a television show, the next football game, shopping for clothes, time with your spouse, the vacation with your kids, or the hunting trip? Now take those things and compare them with how much you look forward to some time alone with God?

Do they even compare? When's the last time you heard yourself say "Honey, I'd like to go to that movie, but I really just want to spend some time in prayer"? How about "you go ahead and start the show, but there's a devotional I'd like to do." Or perhaps "can I do the dishes later, I've been waiting all day to get into the Word." Do these phrases sound foreign to you? Does it seem weird to even read them, like it's a line in a bad movie? Yet, isn't this what we should strive toward? To love God so much we can't wait to spend time with Him. Remember when you were first dating, during that period where all you wanted to do was get away together alone? Where is that passion for God?

> The good man out of the good treasure of his heart brings forth what is good; and the evil man out of the evil treasure brings forth what is evil; for his mouth speaks from that which fills his heart. — (Luke 6:45)

If we want to see what's in our hearts, all we need do is look at what comes out. Are we more critical than we are encouraging? Do we speak hate more than love? Do we speak of our job more than we do of our Lord? Do we even speak of Jesus? At times I have found myself getting fed up with many of the conversations around me as we talked about such unimportant things while my heart just screamed for Jesus.

Search With All Your Heart

We have such an opportunity before us to gain eternal life. There is a God waiting to welcome us into His presence—if only we seek Him out. Jesus taught that we must look past our worldly needs to find what is important.

> And do not seek what you will eat and what you will drink, and do not keep worrying. For all these things the nations of the world eagerly seek; but your Father knows that you need these things. But seek His kingdom, and these things will be added to you.
> — (Luke 12:29–31)

We should first seek His kingdom. When we seek after what God is doing and what He has given, then the things of this world will follow as well. We must learn to seek after the pearl of great price. To give whatever we must to attain this treasure set before us. We need not worry whether it will be worth it or whether we can achieve that which we desire.

> Do not be afraid, little flock, for your Father has chosen gladly to give you the kingdom. — (Luke 12:32)

God wants to give us the kingdom; to open unto us not only His blessings, but also His calling over us. He has a role for each of us to fulfill, a place in this world He created specifically for us. There's a phrase I've heard that I stand by as well, "you're as close to God as you want to be." If we wish to be closer to Him, it is a choice we must make. But to make it, to find God, we must search with our hearts. There isn't a ritual or a prayer to recite that will lead us here.

> For God sees not as man sees, for man looks at the outward appearance, but the Lord looks at the heart. — (1 Samuel 16:7)

It must be with our heart. We can find Him only by searching Him out. Just knowing of God and knowing that we can come to Him doesn't mean we will be different; only that we have the opportunity to be different. The choice is still up to us. The desires of our heart are up to us.

> You will seek Me and find Me when you search for Me with all your heart. — (Jeremiah 29:13)

We can find Him. I'm not talking about the basic faith of believing we are going to heaven; I'm talking about finding God right here in this world. Finding that relationship of love, trust, and friendship. We must come to the simple conclusion that finding this experience with our Lord is worth more than everything else in our lives.

Blessed Are Those Who Hunger

> Blessed are those who hunger and thirst for righteousness, for they shall be satisfied. — (Matthew 5:6)

We will not find satisfaction in our half-hearted devotion to the Lord. Sure, we can appease our conscious for a time, but we won't find happiness there. Do you want to be fulfilled? Do you want to be satisfied with your life? Then you better get hungry for the right things. We treat our spirit just like our physical bodies, where we often fill it with junk food and become malnourished or overweight. The hunger goes away, but our bodies are not satisfied. When our hunger for God surpasses our worldly desires, that is when we can expect to begin finding the Lord. The hard part is to change our hearts. After pushing God away so long, it is tough to make it all about Him again.

> Do not store up for yourselves treasures on earth, where moth and rust destroy, and where thieves break in and steal. But store up for yourselves treasures in heaven, where neither moth nor rust destroys, and where thieves do not break in or steal for where your treasure is, there your heart will be also. — (Matthew 6:19-21)

If we find the things we treasure, whether they be the world or the kingdom, then we find where our heart lies. That means the more we invest our resources in one area, the more we place our heart there. *If you want to change your heart, change your treasure.*

The Word Of God

> For the time will come when they will not endure sound doctrine; but wanting to have their ears tickled, they will accumulate for themselves teachers in accordance to their own desires, and will turn away their ears from the truth and will turn aside to myths.
> — (2 Timothy 4:3–4)

In the year 325 AD, Emperor Constantine brought a group of leaders together to unite the Roman Empire under Christianity at what is known as the Nicaean Council. Constantine had watched the spread of Christianity and wanted to bring it into his empire to unite his people. Many historians view this as a defining moment in Christianity, where it exploded across the world and became a world religion. There are others, however, who look at this as the moment Christianity began to fade; for Constantine was not trying to put the Roman Empire under Christianity, but Christianity under the Roman Empire. To make a religion palatable to all, Constantine and the council combined other religions into Christianity to make their state religion. Unfortunately, Christianity is not something you can put upon a nation or person, it is something God puts upon you. What resulted was a government with control over God's people, who were willing to compromise truth for peace and the leading of the Spirit for the leading of man. For example, do you realize that Easter was named after a "god" who was mentioned in another part of the Bible as a Babylonian god? Did you ever notice that 3 days and nights (as mentioned in Matthew 12:40) after "good Friday" isn't "resurrection Sunday?" Did you realize that Jesus birthday is not actually in December, where it just happens to fall around the winter solstice? Compromising God's ways for "peace" doesn't work. All you need to do is to go read the Old Testament and the compromises Israel made along their journey to see how that worked.

God In A Box

What we find all around us in the church is what I like to call "God in a box." In a similar manner as the Nicaean Council, we will often put our God into a box that makes us more comfortable. I heard a story from a minister who had an interesting encounter with the Lord. The Lord was speaking to him and revealing some new truths that he was having trouble accepting. When it became too much for him, he turned to the Lord and said "I'm sorry, but this just doesn't fit in my doctrine." This is how silly we get, to speak to the Creator about things He has wrong. The Lord very gently responded by saying "I think you need a new doctrine." I have long been concerned that our churches are focused too much upon our doctrines and too little upon the Word of God. In my personal walk it has taken a while, but I've come to the place where if I read something in the Bible which doesn't agree with my beliefs, then I go question my belief. This might seem like an obvious response, but from what I see around me, it's not. How about we just discuss a couple examples.

- Word Over Experience

One simple and very understandable mistake we make is to build our beliefs based upon our experience. This seems reasonable; as it is the manner in which we have come to understand much of the world we live in. This is the basis for the scientific method: go try something, see what happens, and then figure out why. Most of us learn by experience. If I jump in the lake, I sink. Yet, this isn't what happened to Peter. We pray for healing for a family member and they die. How do we resolve this? Should we question if God still heals people? When we read the scripture that tells us to have the elders pray for the sick and they will recover, is that really what it said? Instead of believing, we get creative. Maybe God wanted me sick to teach me a lesson. Maybe my sickness was to reach someone who's lost. Maybe I just sinned and let the devil attack. Soon we find ourselves creating a new doctrine to make sense of what could look like a failure. We would rather have a doctrine to explain away what could be our faults, inadequacies, and lack of understanding. It's as if we can't handle trusting and hoping in only God.

- Spiritual Dyslexia

Spiritual dyslexia is a term I once heard used to explain my next concept. This is where we read a scripture, but understand it backward from what it actually says. We see what we want to see and not what we should. In a non-spiritual perspective, I have seen this at work. One of my developers was working on a problem we've been trying to fix. As he is attempting to fix it, he makes a change and the problem goes away. Once he realized this, he brings that solution to me saying it solved the problem. When I ask why, he tells me because it fixed it. I press him more and find that he can't give me any actual explanation of why it should fix the problem, just that it "did". What he did was take an effect of his change as the resolution of the problem, when it could have been any number of other reasons. Similarly, we often look at scriptures and pick what we think it says and just move on without understanding the why of it. Before I confuse this more, how about an example from John.

If you love me, keep my commands. — (John 14:15)

I found that I've been reading this backward for much of my life. We look at it as "if I love God, I should keep His commands." Then we try to logically work it out. Since I love God, because that's what I'm trying to do, then I need to go do all the things He tells me for this to make sense. Except that's not what this verse said. It's subtle at first, but makes all the difference. The verse did not say that you obey God's commandments to show your love, but that if you loved, you would obey God's commandments. The fact that you don't want to obey is an indication of a lack of love. Why does that make a difference? Because if you obey out of an obligation, you invite bitterness and weariness; as you are doing what you don't want to do. Instead if you are moved out of love for God, you choose to obey because that is what pleases Him. Too often we try to fix problems by understanding, reading, and acting; rather than waiting for God to reveal it to us.

- Don't Want To Pay The Price

Just because we know the truth doesn't mean we're willing to accept it. For example, look at Israel as they stood at the base of Mount Sinai. God just came and showed His glory before them, as He descends upon Mount Sinai in fire. This verse below always brings such sadness into my heart because of how God's people responded.

> All the people perceived the thunder and the lightning flashes and the sound of the trumpet and the mountain smoking; and when the people saw it, they trembled and stood at a distance. Then they said to Moses, "Speak to us yourself and we will listen; but let not God speak to us, or we will die." — (Exodus 20:18-19)

They saw God before them; tangible, real, and frightening. Rather than deal with a living God themselves, they asked Moses to do it. The fear of the Lord came upon them, and they weren't willing to take the chance. Instead, they chose to have Moses talk, and just hear it from him. This saddens me because they had a chance to see God, to be a witness to His glory, and they turned away.

> It is a terrifying thing to fall into the hands of the living God. — (Hebrews 10:31)

Israel was not the only ones guilty of this; we are too. We let the pastors get a word from God to give us, so we can show up at church on Sunday and hear what we need. Rather than go to God ourselves, we ask our leaders to. It may be fear, it may just be laziness, or it may be a lack of time. Whatever the reason, we're willing to let others be an intermediary for us when Jesus has torn open the veil into the inner court. When it comes down to it, we are willing to live our lives without a personal God.

- Willing To Live Without It

Too often we live without truth. We acquire knowledge from church, family, and friends; however, we won't receive it by ourselves. We live wondering why things have happened to us. We wonder if we got sick, would God would help us. We wonder what purpose He has for us. We wonder if we are pleasing to Him. Unfortunately, few of us take the time to find answers. We are comfortable with our homes, our jobs, and our families. We fill up our lives with enough things from the world to quiet those inner voices that cry for something more than ourselves. We take enough of God to feel like we have done the right thing without sacrificing too much.

Truth And Wisdom

I can hear your thoughts.

Ok, maybe I just hear my own. Why should we work so hard? Why is it so important to know truth? Simple, because it is worth it. Seriously. I'm not talking "it will help keep you out of trouble", "it leads you in a good path", or even "it watches after you" type of worth it. I'm talking "find the reason you are alive and become what you could be" worth it. Those people who have found the truth in their lives and lived it, those are the ones that are written about. They are the ones we remember who left their mark on this world.

> *The law of Your mouth is better to me, than thousands of gold and silver pieces.* – Psalm 119:72

What greater truth than the Word of God. His ways are the ways that govern the universe.

> How blessed is the man who finds wisdom and the man who gains understanding. For her profit is better than the profit of silver and her gain better than fine gold. She is more precious than jewels; and nothing you desire compares with her. — (Proverbs 3:13–14)

My personal definition of wisdom is the ability to find truth without experience. An experienced man finds it after the first try. A wise man finds the correct path on the first try. Wisdom is the finding of truth and understanding it, which is worth more than gold. We must come to the attitude that we want truth more than anything else. Not only that, but we're willing to accept truth no matter what we feel about it. This is important as we often have our own ideas and God has to clean them up. I think I can sum up where I'm headed with a couple excerpts from John 6.

> Truly, truly, I say to you, unless you eat the flesh of the Son of Man and drink His blood, you have no life in yourselves…
>
> Therefore many of His disciples, when they heard this said, "This is a difficult statement; who can listen to it?"…
>
> As a result of this many of His disciples withdrew and were not walking with Him anymore. So Jesus said to the twelve, "You do not want to go away also, do you?" Simon Peter answered Him, "Lord, to whom shall we go? You have words of eternal life. — (John 6:53,60,66–68)

Here the Lord made a statement that still perplexes many of us to this day. Eat His flesh? Drink His blood? Sounds more like a horror movie than a Bible story. Many of those following Him had the same reaction. When they realized that they couldn't make sense of His words, they left. The disciples remained. Peter's reaction is still one of my favorite responses in the Bible. In my words, Peter's response was, "Lord, I don't get it, but I know you have truth so where else would I go?" Peter knew that truth was more important than what he wanted or believed.

God's measurements for qualifying people are different than ours. The disciples could recognize the truth, even though I doubt they could understand it at the time. Perhaps this is what qualified them to be His disciples, their willingness to accept truth and follow it. Jesus wasn't interested in the crowds, the fanfare, or being a celebrity. He was interested in the truth and true disciples.

One of the most important conclusions you can reach early in your relationship with Christ is to accept His Word as truth above your beliefs. This is one of those statements you need to think about. It seems perfectly logical, until you go deep. There are many lifestyles and beliefs that our society wants to force upon us. In the name of tolerance, they push their beliefs upon the rest of the world. Strange thing is, if I were to go based solely upon myself, I would want to agree in different areas, especially as I have friends and coworkers leading lifestyles "against" scripture. It's not up to me though, because I'm not God. So, when I read in the Bible that a certain thing is wrong; I accept that. It doesn't matter what I feel or what my beliefs are; if it's in the Word, then it's true. Rather than taking what I read and filtering it through what I believe to be right, I will take what is written and filter my beliefs through that. If I am wrong, I must change. This is one of those places that our denominations have gotten off track. We take our stands upon what creeds we've created, rather than upon the Word of God. We would rather be told what to believe, than to meditate upon the Word until we understand. If you wish to mature, you must take God's Word for what it is, accept it no matter what it says, and be willing to change your mind. Why? Because guess what, you're probably wrong on a lot of things.

We can make our beliefs into whatever we want, but if our house is to stand, we must base ourselves upon the whole truth and not only the part of the truth we're comfortable with. In 2 Samuel 21,

God told David that Saul's treatment of the Gibeonites had led to a famine, which led to David having to hand over seven of Saul's descendants to be killed to make up for Saul's sin. These people did nothing themselves to deserve death that I can see; they didn't even have a choice in the matter. The fairness center of me cries out that this was wrong, and yet this act ended the famine that God had allowed. I can't disregard the truth of God's nature just because it doesn't make appease my sensibilities.

But there's even more to it than that. Truth is more than just knowing what happened; it's knowing what is truly at work. How do I describe this? Let's use sickness as an example. One day, Jesus went to Peter's house where He healed Peter's mother-in-law and all the others who came to Him sick. It was said that this was to fulfill the prophecy that *"He himself took our infirmities and carried away our diseases"* (Matthew 8:17). The truth here is that Jesus came to take away our diseases. With this in mind, if I find myself sick and after prayer I'm not well, does that invalidate this truth? No. We see truths in scripture such as Jesus wanting to heal the sick, but since it didn't happen for us, we build a doctrine to explain it away. The truth of the spirit supersedes our reality. That's how Peter could walk on water when Jesus said so. The physical world had to comply when Jesus spoke.

The Root Of Truth

What is truth? Truth is not merely knowledge. Truth is not what we read in a book and hear from a teacher. We have so much access to knowledge and yet so little understanding. It has become too easy to look for books and pastors to tell us what we should believe, rather than finding it for ourselves. Truth is not found in our doctrines, because truth is not a concept but a person — Jesus Christ. He is the Living Word. Not only does He embody truth, He is truth. We have a tendency of too quickly trying to capture our belief in words rather than capturing the person of our beliefs. A relationship takes much more work than a document. We find comfort in having someone lead us and tell us the truth, but don't want to take the time to make Jesus that person for us.

> And I saw heaven opened, and behold, a white horse, and He who sat on it is called Faithful and True, and in righteousness He judges and wages war. His eyes are a flame of fire, and on His head are many diadems; and He has a name written on Him which no one knows except Himself. He is clothed with a robe dipped in blood, and His name is called The Word of God. — (Revelation 19:11–13)

Jesus is the Word of God. What does that mean? That every passage in the Bible reads Jesus. Much as Jesus was the express image of the Father, Jesus is also the Word of God made into flesh. When we come to find truth in the Word, we need to find Jesus. Jesus is not necessarily what we want Him to be, but as our Lord, we follow Him. This is a bit of a tough concept to explain, but you need to find the feeling and truth behind what the Bible says.

The Living Word

As we continue talking about the "Word", we need to understand a little more what that word means. Let's start with the two Greek words used for "The Word" in the New Testament: logos and rhema. The logos typically refers to the written word. I say "typically" because it has much more depth to it. For now, we'll keep it simple as the written word; that which is laid out before us. Jesus was the logos. He was the word of God laid out in front of us for us to read and understand.

> For the word of God is living and active, sharper than any two-edged sword, piercing to the division of soul and of spirit, of joints and of marrow, and discerning

the thoughts and intentions of the heart. — (Hebrews 4:12)

Now for the second term used for the Word, rhema. Rhema translates to the spoken word.

> And Mary said, "Behold, I am the servant of the Lord; let it be to me according to your word." And the angel departed from her. — (Luke 1:38)

In this verse, the translation for "word" is rhema. The difference is that the angel is speaking a word that came from God for Mary, and not the written law or scripture. Does this make it any less a word of God because it wasn't something in their law at the time? Sometimes we fear to take any word as coming from God unless it's in the Bible; however, much of what God did in the Bible was through his Rhema word. The prophets and apostles often got a rhema word from the Lord, the Holy Spirit, or angels to give them direction. This was a major part of the success with their ministry in Acts. The Lord directed them on where to go and where to not go. You can look at the time Peter was told to meet Cornelius (Acts 10:19-20), or when Philip was told to meet the Ethiopian man (Acts 8:26). In both cases the word of God came to these disciples and specifically led them. Even Jesus said He would only speak of that which He heard from the Father (John 12:49). Jesus also followed the guidance of the rhema word of God.

This is an area we need to be careful. Most Pentecostals have no problem here, but a lot of Evangelicals do. I have heard it taught that once we received the Bible, God had no need to directly speak anymore. I also had a friend once sit me down concerned because I was expecting that God would speak directly to me. He said that it's only certain special people that God would speak to who have that need, it's not for all of us. I have a tough time reading about something that God would do for others and say we should have, only to explain it away as not for me. It's hard reading that "God does not show favoritism" (Acts 10:34), and then believe He will limit my relationship with Him. Even more than that, I read that "my sheep hear my voice" (John 10:27), but I am told that I cannot hear from Him. This sort of limiting our relationship with God comes down to either trusting our experiences or a lack of hunger. That might seem a little harsh, but like I said, I'm on a search for truth, not for what makes me feel the best.

We Need Revelation

Next, we need to discuss an important aspect of truth which took me years to understand.

> When Jesus came to the region of Caesarea Philippi, he asked his disciples, "Who do people say the Son of Man is?" They replied, "Some say John the Baptist; others say Elijah; and still others, Jeremiah or one of the prophets." "But what about you?" he asked. "Who do you say I am?" Simon Peter answered, "You are the Messiah, the Son of the living God." Jesus replied, "Blessed are you, Simon son of Jonah, for this was not revealed to you by flesh and blood, but by my Father in heaven. — (Matthew 16:13–17)

We know the disciples have heard Jesus say that He was the Son of God. They also heard what the demons called Jesus as they were cast out. By now, you might think that they would figure it out themselves; yet when Peter answered Jesus's question, Jesus responded to him with words that may seem odd at first glance? He said it was revealed to Peter by the Father. This is one of those things that I just glazed over as a "that's a weird statement" in my younger days. If Peter had heard this, why would Jesus say it that way? Because Peter spoke in truth, and truth can only be received through revelation from the Father. There are two common words for knowledge used in the Bible. Gnosis which is what I would call head knowledge, and epignosis which is a deeper sort of experiential knowledge. You can spend your days memorizing the Bible, but until God gives you revelation and makes it come alive, it won't change you.

> But a natural man does not accept the things of the Spirit of God, for they are foolishness to him; and he cannot understand them, because they are spiritually appraised. — (1 Corinthians 2:14)

We can hear truth, but that doesn't mean we understand. I can tell you how much God loves me, but that doesn't mean I know it. If we receive a revelation of God's love, we won't be so easily shaken. When someone runs into our car, instead of being angry we would be understanding. We wouldn't lose our temper, despair, or give up. If we knew how much God loved us, all these things would be but little specks upon a life so blessed by the Lord we would barely take notice. What's a dent in my car compared to the incalculable love of Christ.

Revelation comes from God. It comes when we seek Him and seek His truth. We can't just go and capture it ourselves, we need it to be revealed to us. I can tell you from experience how much good knowledge does. I've always been a big reader and listener to Christian teachers. Through books I've acquired much knowledge, but that knowledge never made me come alive. It's a good base for the revelation to take advantage of, but until I started getting revelation, my life wouldn't change. You see this truth, when it becomes a part of you, can't help but change you. This is why I tend to cringe when my church does a reading plan. What good does reading through three to four chapters a day if it doesn't speak to me. Some days I only make it through a couple verses before I must stop as God's starting to speak to me. If I had to read multiple chapters, I may have to turn God away to get my reading done.

> Man does not live be bread alone, but by every word that comes from the mouth of God. — (Matthew 4:4)

We have undervalued the truth. I guess we feel like we understand enough to pull things off, when in fact we need more truth. The truth of God supersedes this world. When you get hold of a truth, it can not only change your life, but those around us. Instead, we're willing to live with less. When you read from the Bible, the Word of God gives you revelation. That revelation has a power inside it; the power to live according to God's word. That power can change you and make you something new.

Bread Of Life

> Do not work for the food which perishes, but for the food which endures to eternal life, which the Son of Man will give to you, for on Him the Father, God, has set His seal. — (John 6:27)

This verse brings to mind the story of Jesus and the Samaritan woman in John 4. She came to the well for water, most likely having walked for miles, and at this point Jesus tells her that she should ask for living water. You can imagine, after spending so much time carrying a pot and water back and forth, Jesus's analogy was meant to show her how much better living water would be. Similarly, we spend a great amount of effort working for things in this natural world that will pass away. Our house will get old, our food will be eaten, and our clothes will wear out. If our work is only for this world, our efforts are wasted. Jesus tells us that instead we should work for the food which endures; the food that He can give us. Don't make the mistake here of assuming that this only speaks of treasures we will receive in heaven. Where do we find this food, and perhaps more importantly, what is it? If we are told to work for this food from God, then perhaps we better understand what it is.

> For the bread of God is that which comes down out of heaven, and gives life to the world. — (John 6:33)

The Jesus We Forgot

Bread is one of the most common foods mentioned in the Bible. Frequently you will find it is used in place of the word food. In this case, I interpret "bread" as just food in general. Hunger is our body telling us we need more food to keep going. Bread, or food, gives life to our bodies. It provides the energy and sustenance to keep us going and the strength we need to grow. Unfortunately, too many of us stay spiritually malnourished. We don't see in the spirit to realize how bad off we are, but the signs are evident. We are constantly looking for things around us to fill the hunger. We desire excitement, love, entertainment, or anything else we can come up with to fill our "stomachs". I want to be clear that this isn't necessarily us looking for salvation, but rather the hunger for life. Our desires give away our heart. Look to what you fill your free time with. When you take time off from work, family, kids, and responsibilities, where do you go? Do you head to the movies, pick up a book, or take a trip? When you find a break what do you reach for?

> My eyes anticipate the night watches, That I may meditate on Your word. — (Psalm 119:148)

This verse hit me deeply when the Spirit brought it to my attention. David puts me to shame. He was excited to get the night shift. Seriously? How can you be excited to stay up overnight watching over the walls for an enemy to possibly come? David could do this with excitement because he loved God's word. He looked forward to those nights where he could sit alone and think upon the word of God. Here we find a lost art among much of the church — meditation. We've let other religions take meditation and turn it into something not of the Lord. We think of meditation and imagine monks in the lotus position or chanting druids. Keep in mind, the devil does not create. Instead he takes truth and perverts it into something he can use. Many of these practices that happen in other religions are things that God began, but were perverted into idolatry. We need to rediscover meditation. The core of meditating upon the Word of God is to take the Word and just mull it over. Speak it out, repeat it in your mind, think on it, and imagine it. In essence, pour time into it. I'm not talking a minute or two, but a long time on a verse or passage. Often I will take a short passage which I have memorized and spend an hour and a half while I mow my yard meditating upon it. In the process, I get more out of that passage than I ever did sitting quietly in my chair with my reading plan. It takes time to clear you mind of all the other junk and soak in the Word. There is a place in our relationship with the Lord where we need to be alone and quietly meditate on the Word in stillness, but first I am more concerned that you learn to meditate upon them however you can. When you take the time to consider each part, focus on it, and clear your mind of other concerns, the Holy Spirit can reveal new nuggets of truth to you. Ironically, this act has become a little frustrating to me at times, because I tend to stay upon a passage much longer than I used to. For example, my quiet times have been working my way through Romans, slowly, for weeks, and I'm still not done. Often, I only make it a few verses in a sitting because there is just so much to be learned as I meditate upon them. This practice irritates my "religious" side which expects to read chapters at a time.

> Your words were found and I ate them, And Your words became for me a joy and the delight of my heart; For I have been called by Your name. — (Jeremiah 15:16)

God's word is our food. We need to come into a new level of appreciation for the Bible. We know it's God's Word, but we relegate it to such a small portion of our day. Instead we should be taking it with us everywhere. It is the word of life. Keep it always upon your heart, on your lips, and in your mind.

> Neither have I gone back from the commandment of his lips; I have esteemed the words of his mouth more than my necessary food. — (Job 23:12)

When's the last time that you skipped a meal to read the word of

God? Have you ever? Eating food is so routine for my body, when I skip a meal my body makes it painfully clear that I did. Now, if I were to miss reading the word for a day, would I notice? Does my spirit get weak and tell me to get some food? Do I realize that I don't have the energy I should and go find it by eating from the Word? For most of my life the answer was no which tells me a lot about how I was living.

Most of Our Battles Are for Truth

One of our biggest battle-grounds is that of truth. You can trace many of our issues back to us believing or accepting a lie rather than the truth.

> When anyone hears the word of the kingdom and does not understand it, the evil one comes and snatches away what has been sown in his heart. — (Matthew 13:19)

The devil wants to steal away all truth from us as soon as it comes. Look around and you can see how he's distorted truth. He's taken compassion and turned it into tolerance, hard work into greediness, love into desire, etc. The devil will pluck away all the good things in our life that he can.

The church has been struggling to find truth again after so long with so little. How else can you describe the dark ages. The "church" was blocking truth from getting to the people. They were using their spiritual authority to hold power over the people. Since then we've been getting waves of truth coming back. The reformation brought back salvation through grace, then sanctification was introduced, the Spirit and so much more. Since then, God has continued to reveal more truth to those who are able to receive them.

> He who has ears to hear, let him hear. — (Matthew 11:15)

The truth will set us free.

Knowing God

Faith In A God We Don't Know

There is a belief I have seen among many believers in the church that worries me. What I have noticed are a people who are willing to know of God, but unwilling to know Him. They take what they read in their Bible and what they hear taught by others to create their own understanding of who they think Jesus is. They build a view of Jesus in their minds; based off the knowledge they have accumulated and the understanding that they have, and make decisions using that. They are willing to listen to people tell them how much their God loves them, but not willing to experience it themselves. They see how God likes to bless His children, but see only the outward expressions of it. They look for the scripture and the action that leads to the response they want. If they want to be blessed, they pray like Jabez. If they want security, they pray Psalm 91. They have been told how to handle their situations by others, and as they continue to act in the methods they've been taught, they create a system for how God works and what it takes for His rewards.

Inevitable, their god will fail them. Calamity comes along and they can't understand how their loving god would let that happen to them. For example, they can't understand why they can't find a job, because their view of God is someone who will take care of all their physical needs first. They put everything into their family, believing that a loving God wouldn't let something happen, so when it does they fall apart. They make financial decisions based off a belief that God prospers His own, and find themselves overwhelmed in debt. When their model of God fails, they don't know what to believe.

Too many of us have created an idol as our own god. An idol of our beliefs is as real as an idol of gold. It is easier to create a god that covers our comfort and fits into what we want to believe, than to come to know a God that may not believe as we do. Paul described people who do this as "holding to a form of godliness, although they have denied its power" (2 Timothy 3:1). At a men's conference I attended, I remember one of the speakers saying: "One day I realized that God and I were incompatible, and one of us had to change." Whether it be a golden Buddha, or a mental Jesus; when we put our faith in what we understand, we set our path to failure. Faith must be in a person, and not a belief.

We Can Know God

What should be one of the most important truths of Christianity is that we can know God. Let me be clear here. I don't mean the "spiritual knowing God" that we sometimes assign, where we know of Him, have fleeting impressions of direction, and have an occasional verse come to mind when we need it. That is not knowing God. I mean knowing Him like we do family. The kind of knowing where we see them often, talk on the phone, send funny messages during the day, rely upon them for advice, and spend our time with them. We too often think of God as that big entity way up there in the sky that we can never understand. This view is not scriptural.

> I am the good shepherd, and I know my own and My own know me. — (John 10:14)

Jesus taught that His sheep would know Him. Surely, we can be as good as sheep. How did the sheep know their shepherd? They knew him by how he looked, his voice, his smell, and even the way he walked. Jesus came to earth to show us the way back to the Father. We can know Him, not just in knowledge, but in person.

> Behold, I stand at the door and knock; if anyone hears My voice and opens the door, I will come in to him and will dine with him, and he with Me. — (Revelation 3:20)

The way has been set and our Lord is waiting for us. God provided everything we need, which leads us back to a core truth.

> Draw near to God and He will draw near to you. — (James 4:8)

We are as close to God as we want to be.

We have nothing to do with being saved, but everything to do with how close we come to God. Salvation has opened the way, but we must walk into it. In the end, we initiate the closeness in the relationship. It's up to us to really dig into God. We must desire the relationship more than anything else. We pursue Him as we would a lover. If we draw near, God is faithful to come close as well. He stands at the door and knocks, but we must let Him in. God will rarely force Himself upon us.

We Have A Choice

> Then they said to Moses, "Speak to us yourself and we will listen; but let not God speak to us, or we will die." — (Exodus 20:19)

Israel was afraid of God and sent Moses to the mountain rather than coming themselves. Just as Israel did, so do we. We are happy to go to our churches and listen to our preachers, read our Christian devotionals, and do our quiet times; however, we aren't willing to come before a holy God. We know deep down that to do so means to admit things we aren't ready to. We like our lives as they are. We like how things are going, and most of all, we like our control. To stand before God, knowing the earth is just His footstool, is to validate to ourselves that we are nothing and our lives are just a puff of air. Most of us cannot handle that. So, we send our preachers to God. We let others spend the time to find truth and regurgitate it to us like a mother bird feeding her young. We do our scheduled quiet times, but are unwilling to sit as Jesus's feet like Mary who forgot all her other cares. It's easier to allow someone else to tell us what they hear, and hope that it covers our inadequacies.

No. We must come to God ourselves. We need to humble ourselves and know that without Him, we are nothing. We should sacrifice whatever it takes to please Him, for that is what really matters. We need to make knowing Him a priority over all the other things in our lives. What are we to gain if we live our life our way, and at the end find God desired more.

God Is A Person

The first truth upon this path is to understand that God is a person. I know that may sound odd. By this I don't mean that He is human, but that He has an identity. He has thoughts, emotions, and desires. We need to treat Him more like a person and less like a grocery store. So often we come to God with our problems and our needs, but don't ever come to Him otherwise. For example, one day at work I walked up to a co-worker of mine to ask her a question. As soon as I got there, she turned to me and said, "Oh no, not you. Every time you come to me you have a problem." I had never even realized this was the case. I had gotten so caught up in my work that I hadn't noticed this was the only time I went to her. She was hesitant to see me because she knew why I came. Now consider how God feels when you come to Him? Do you think He cringes because He knows you're about to ask for help like always, or does He smile and welcome a friend with whom He often talks?

Don't fear, God wants time with you because He loves you and created you. Spending time with God is, of course, not the same as walking down the aisle to get to know that coworker nearby. Even so, it shouldn't be any harder. Our experience tells us otherwise because of the barriers we've put in the way. I've heard it said that we treat God as a tour guide of our lives, hoping that He'll show us all the good things we could see in this world. Perhaps that's why we get so upset when things fall apart? We have a tendency to look at our life as all the things He can give us and not what we can give Him.

Eternal life is in our relationship with God and not in the things He has given us.

Have you ever asked God how He felt? Or perhaps, have you ever asked God how His day was going? I have. It had never dawned on me to even think about Him this way for a long time. I come to Him for advice, for help, and for strength. I just never thought about reciprocating those actions. I would worship Him and do things for Him, but I saw those as my duties, not as my heart. After hearing about a minister recounting an experience along these lines, I realized that I had not thought about God in that manner, as a person with feelings and desires. So, one day I began to ask Him how He is doing, and the most amazing thing happened. He answered. Not all the time(in fact only sometimes), but one time in particular I remember because of what He told me. He said that He was sad as He has provided so much for His children but they were content with so little. Think of it this way, God gave us a huge basket of fruit, and all we ever eat are the grapes. He had paid for all these wonderful gifts that we have let waste away. We get salvation, but never fully realize the eternal life He has provided. This made Him sad. Next time your mind is still and your heart is open, remember this and ask God. See what He will tell you.

Who Are We Then?

Let's talk about how we can get to know God better. Sometimes the best answers are the simplest ones. If we just thought about getting to know a regular person, how would we go about getting to know them? We can start by learning of them from others, but the best methods to get to know someone is to spend time with them, ask them questions, and do things with them. Why not do this with the Lord?

Time To Read

First, we learn about Him. If I wanted to know about Thomas

Jefferson, I would look him up on the internet, then maybe buy some books written about him. I could consult with people I know who like history and have studied him. We can do the same for God. Find people whom you respect and ask them. Go to a book store and look for books about God. Most of all, read His word. We have a Bible full of scriptures about Him, from Him, and to Him. We can see how God acted with others and learn things about His nature.

> For whatever was written in earlier times was written for our instruction, so that through perseverance and the encouragement of the Scriptures we might have hope. — (Romans 15:4)

We can look to what happened with Israel, the prophets, the apostles, and others to see how God works with man. We can read through the Bible and see what He did, but perhaps the best way is to look at Jesus.

> Remember those who led you, who spoke the word of God to you; and considering the result of their conduct, imitate their faith. Jesus Christ is the same yesterday and today and forever. — (Hebrews 13:7–8)

Because Jesus is the same, we can see how God has worked with those who came before us. Jesus said Himself that He only did what He saw the Father doing (John 5:19). Think about that. If Jesus only did what He saw the Father doing, then you can find out what God is like and what He does by looking at what Jesus did. Look through His life and see how He acted and how He spoke to others, because He did everything like the Father. That is a wonderful thing for us in the New Testament church, because we can look to see how Jesus acted, and know that God does the same. We can listen to Jesus's words and know that these are the words of the Father.

Operator, Can You Connect Me To God

Knowing about God is an important step, but knowing of Him does not mean we know Him. Just because I know where you were born, where you went to school, the church you attended, and what kind of car you have; that doesn't mean I actually know you. It may give me ideas about you and about your nature; however, I can't build a relationship on ideas. The best way for me to get to know you is to talk with you. You may be thinking, "of course, we have to pray to get to know God, but it's still hard since I don't hear his responses." This is I suspect the single biggest hurdle for Christians. We know how to talk to God, but not how to listen.

Before I take you any farther, we need to get one thing straight. Do you know that God will talk to you? Do you believe that the God of the universe will take a second to say something to you? I am convinced that many Christians believe this in theory, but when it comes down to it, they don't expect it to happen. This mindset isn't what Jesus taught.

> My sheep hear My voice, and I know them, and they follow Me. — (John 10:27)

I remember my dad telling me the story about how this verse came alive to Him. One day it dawned on him that God speaks to His sheep, and that he — my dad — was one of those sheep. Every day after this realization, he would spend time praying and thanking God that His sheep hear His voice. Then one day, he heard His voice. You see, God speaks to us. He wants to guide, correct, and love us. He didn't drop us here to be on our own. Some people want to think that we have the Bible and have no need to hear from God. Again, this is not what Jesus taught. As Jesus neared the crucifixion, He spoke to His disciples concerning when He would leave them. One of the many things He told them is that the Spirit would come to guide them.

> But the Helper, the Holy Spirit, whom the Father will send in My name, He will teach you all things, and bring to your remembrance all that I said to you.
> — (John 14:26)

So tell me, how can the Holy Spirit teach us all things if He isn't talking to us? Jesus continued:

> But when He, the Spirit of truth, comes, He will guide you into all the truth; for He will not speak of His own initiative, but whatever He hears, He will speak; and He will disclose to you what is to come. He will glorify Me, for He will take of Mine, and will disclose it to you. — (John 16:14–15)

The Holy Spirit will speak to us on behalf of Jesus. It is amazing that God would choose to speak to us. Unfortunately, I have found even in my own life that it can be more convenient for me to make a doctrine based off of my experience rather than learning to hear from the one who is truth.

Hearing Is Important

Hearing God's voice is critical for us to walk in His ways. Jesus was up front with the fact that He only did and said what He received from the Father. Hearing from God will give us better results than doing it on our own. Take for example the disciples fishing. They had spent all day fishing and didn't catch anything, but when Jesus tells them where to throw the nets; their nets begin to tear from the size of the catch. In one instance of obedience, they caught more fish than they were able to in a day of their own attempts. I am convinced that few hear His voice well, but those that do can change many lives by moving when God says to.

Have you ever heard one of those stories where someone is at the end of their rope with nowhere to turn, then a stranger shows up and says something like "God told me to give this to you," providing them with exactly what they needed? How would that affect their faith in God to provide? God loves to do these sorts of things. Remember the coin in the fish with Jesus, the donkey that hadn't be ridden, or the upper room that just happened to be prepared? The problem isn't God's willingness, but our ability to hear. Rather than going out throwing that fishing lure one hundred times into the water, instead if you hear the Lord say "over there," you can toss the net in and catch a bunch of fish at once. How much more productive and useful could you be to Him then?

On a more selfish note, He also protects us. For you parents, how many times have you warned your children about a danger. Whether it be a hot stove or a car in the street, you want your children to be attentive to your voice so you can protect them from bad things. God also wants to do the same way. He's given us His teaching, but He also wants to provide direction. He'll guide us in our everyday decisions if we let Him.

Can You Hear Me Now?

Too often I hear about Christians who feel like God isn't talking to them. They spend consistent time asking God questions, but hearing nothing in return. I suspect that's where most of us spend our time. We pray at our meals, sit in church, and try to read our Bibles, but still feel lost. Why then don't we hear God speaking? I've heard it compared to a radio signal. When you turn your radio on and nothing comes through, what do you blame it on? Do you immediately blame it on the station? No, most likely it's a fault with your equipment. The chances of a station suddenly not broadcasting are pretty low. Even more, what's the chance that God can't get through? Most likely the problem is that your antennae is not plugged in, tuned to the correct signal, or out of range of the station. I'm not saying that He answers every question we ask, but He's communicating much more than we're receiving. Here are some reasons I've found that we don't hear.

We Choose Not To Listen

When we choose to ignore God, we put up a wall. If God has spoken to us, asking us to do something and we ignored Him, He tends to get a little quieter. Why should we expect God to speak with us when we haven't listened in the past? We cannot pick and choose which messages from God we will accept. Rebellion to God is rebellion, no matter how we feel about it. Still, God is a gentlemen. If you tell Him to go away enough, He will. For this reason, if you hear His voice and set it aside enough times, you will stop hearing Him.

We Don't Stop And Listen

Don't cheat God out of blessing you. He wants to talk with you, so don't keep your mind occupied such that you don't have the time to stop and listen. Let me tell you a typical day I used to have. I would wake in the morning with just enough time to shower and get ready for work. Then, I'd hop into my car for the 30-minute drive and start my audio book—it's a sci-fi story. Did I mention I like some science fiction? I would get to work and work hard. I'm a pretty focused guy, so I don't take smoke breaks or do much chit chat during the day. Sometimes coworkers will come up and we would discuss non-work things, but even then, I don't let it go long. During times where I'd get overwhelmed, I would bring up a news website or a comic for a couple minutes, then get back to work. Lunch hits, sometimes I'd go out with others, other times I would just need a break from people so I'd eat and listen to my book. It's a good one. Continue working till end of my time, drive home, and yet again, audio book. Reach home, work out. Guess what I would listen to as I ran? You got it. Head out to eat with my wife. We discuss work, friends, etc. Come home, turn on tv for one of our shows. We nearly always have a couple shows waiting on us. Do some house work, sit and read a book (different story) as I wind down before bed. Go to bed. Repeat. Since I began this book, I've added a child, which means I have taken away a couple of the "for me" things, and added a lot more play time, school prep, food prep and other tasks. In one day I have filled my head with a days worth of work, at least one fictional book, probably some Barbie play-time, and possibly a TV show. If God were to say something to me, would I even notice?

Be still and know that I am God. — (Psalm 46:10)

God could overwhelm us. He could raise His voice and drown out the universe, but He doesn't. If He wanted to, He could stand up and yell; then all the world would fall to its knees. Someday that will happen. As for today, God wants friends, not prisoners. If He were to flex His muscles for us, what choice would be left? He doesn't want us as a prisoner with no choices, but as a people with free will. To this purpose, He doesn't yell. If we stop to listen long enough, He is there and waiting.

We Listen But Can't Pick Out His Voice

Still, even when we stop to listen, we may find that we can no longer hear His voice. This loss of hearing usually has less to do with God and more to do with us. Let me give you an example of what I'm trying to say first. There's this game I've played before, it's one of those typical relay race games you find at a children's summer camp. There are two people on each team that are playing at a time, one team member is blindfolded, and the other is standing at the finish line. The blindfolded one follows the directions of their teammate to avoid obstacles and make it to the finish line. The problem is, the other teams are yelling as well. To win the race, the blindfolded teammate has to listen to their team and not the others, trusting their teammate to guide them correctly. You can imagine what happens when they don't listen to their teammate. First, they begin wandering in a not-so-straight line, and then typically run into something that will trip them up. Often, they will fall down and completely lose track of which direction they should be going. The farther off track they get, the harder it becomes to hear their teammate since they've moved farther away. And if they stop listening for just a minute, they might forget which voice is their teammate's and then they've truly lost.

Remember all those things I've filled my life with? Guess what that does for hearing God. It's like the story above. There are so many voices, the more you pay attention to one, the better you hear. God's voice is often a still small voice. He speaks to our spirit through the Holy Spirit.

> But the Helper, the Holy Spirit, whom the Father will send in My name, He will teach you all things, and bring to your remembrance all that I said to you.
> — (John 14:26)

There are a lot of things crying out for the attention of your mind. Here's a quick exercise to show you this. I want you to look at the time, then close your eyes and just quietly focus upon Jesus and nothing else. Clear your mind of all thoughts and words, then just love Jesus. Now, see how long you can hold that before another thought comes in. If you made it for a minute, that is really good. Most likely you will last less than that. I think I made it for 20 seconds the first time I did that. Our minds don't know how to be still. We will address this more in a later chapter.

He Speaks To Us, But We Don't Value His Words

Let's take that next step. Let's say your spouse has asked you to help them remember to water the plants later tonight. I am not sure about the rest of you reading this, but I suspect my wife is probably rolling her eyes already. I'm notorious for her asking me to remember something, and saying I'll help, only to forget. Sometimes I just don't value what she says above what I'm doing. I tell her yes, because that's the right thing to say and I truly mean to help, but then in my mind I don't give it enough importance. This is usually not a conscious decision, but rather more like a habit. Because of this, I often let her down. I'm actually surprised she still asks me to help her remember things. In this case I have shown that I don't value her words by not remembering them. Similarly, we prove that we don't value God's words by not following them. James says it this way:

> But prove yourselves doers of the word, and not merely hearers who delude themselves. For if anyone is a hearer of the word and not a doer, he is like a man who looks at his natural face in a mirror; for once he has looked at himself and gone away, he has immediately forgotten what kind of person he was.
> — (James 1:22–24)

I have done something similar with books many times; especially back in school when I was studying for a test. I could find myself reading a page 3 or 4 times, each time realizing I have no idea what I just read. I would read through the words, but without thinking about them, it was all nonsense. My mind was focused upon something else and it just all got lost. The same for the man in the mirror, he goes to look at himself to see what he looks like, then moves away so quickly he forgets. Not only was it a waste of time, but he still doesn't even know what he looks like. We should try our best every time we hear from the Lord to figure out how to use it and what it's for, because God has an order to things. There is a reason He shows us what He does, and if we miss out on one lesson, we're ill-prepared for the next.

To This One

> Thus says the LORD,
> 'Heaven is My throne and the earth is My footstool
> Where then is a house you could build for Me?
> And where is a place that I may rest?
> For My hand made all these things,
> Thus all these things came into being,' declares the LORD
> 'But to this one I will look,
> To him who is humble and contrite of spirit, and who trembles at My word.' — (Isaiah 66:1–2)

After God set us in our place by showing where He stands, He let us know the type of person who can catch His attention. He pays attention to the one that is humble and trembles at His word. Over and over I will return to this same point—He is God. Our little brains just can't seem to make that connection often enough. Now, let me ask you an important question, do you tremble when God speaks to you? When you hear His word, does it shake you up? I can say that for most of my life, it didn't. I can find myself reading from the Bible and treating it as a nice story with a good lesson, rather than the Word of God which created the universe. How can someone take a truth from the creator of the universe, and treat it like a nice fortune cookie. How foolish we are. Remember that story where I was walking into work and God spoke to me. That time I got it. I was shaking the rest of the way to my desk. I understood that the God of the universe had stopped to correct this little speck called me.

Do not speak in the hearing of a fool, for he will despise the wisdom of your words. - Proverbs 23:9.

If we are foolish and don't honor His words, why should God continue to speak with us? It is a waste. Fortunately for us, God is gracious. He does not give up so quickly on us as we deserve. He's not off throwing a fit like a child who decides that since their sibling isn't listening to them, they won't talk anymore. Unfortunately, I see too many of us who still seem to think that this tactic works with others. Luckily for us, God will continue to speak to us, hoping that we will listen.

You will seek Me and find Me when you search for Me with all your heart – Jeremiah 29:13

To find the Lord takes all our heart. He doesn't reward the half-hearted, the ones that look for Him in their spare time. He's a jealous God. He wants our full attention. Somehow, we've convinced ourselves that showing up to church, saying a couple words before meals, and giving the last of our day to Him is enough. We believe that second-best and left-overs are enough to appease the Ancient of Days. Maybe we should learn from the lesson of the Laodiceans.

> I know your deeds, that you are neither cold nor hot; I wish that you were cold or hot. So because you are lukewarm, and neither hot nor cold, I will spit you out of My mouth. — (Revelation 3:15-16)

We cannot have it both ways. Here's a saying I think is fitting here: "If you can live with less of God, you will".

Getting Down To It

Now that I've spoken of many reasons as to why you may not be hearing God's voice, let's talk about practical ways to begin again. We begin with the Bible. The Bible is wonderful because you know it's His word. Read His word and think about it. This is the primary form of communication that many of us use. There are so many decisions in life that the Bible can answer immediately, but you need to put them into practice. Look for scriptures that speak about issues you're dealing with. The words of God are our bread, and we need food for each day to grow. Don't get caught up in a reading plan or a set goal. Read until God speaks to you. If you do that, you will be changed.

Don't read the Bible like a book on etiquette, where we look for the rules to follow and words to find comfort, but don't look for God himself. Reading with just our mind can only give us so much. How are we to interpret what we read? How are we to understand what the Lord has done without guidance? Jesus didn't tell His disciples that He was sending them a book to teach them, but the Spirit, which would "guide them into all truth". For the Word to come alive, we need to hear from the Spirit.

One truth I learned from the Spirit as a teenager was to follow God's peace. As I was finishing high school, I had to make a decision concerning which college I should go to. This isn't something I can go to the Bible and find a verse to tell me what to do. I needed to hear from the Lord. So, I gave it to Him. I went to God in prayer and told Him that I didn't know what to do, and most importantly that I wanted to do what He had in mind for me. I didn't hear a voice or receive an answer that day; in fact, I never received a concrete answer. As the weeks went by of me praying and waiting on the Lord, I found that I knew the answer. After the fact, I realized I had learned a truth from this verse.

> Be anxious for nothing, but in everything by prayer and supplication with thanksgiving let your requests be made known to God. And the peace of God, which surpasses all comprehension, will guard your hearts and your minds in Christ Jesus. — (Philippians 4:6-7)

His peace directed me. It was sort of gradual, as I found myself leaning toward a certain path over time. After a while, I found I reached the point where I knew it was the right place. This won't work when your desires are too strong for one of the choices, as you will confuse that with God's direction. However, if you can step out of the decision and make it His, you can find peace in knowing that He had a say in it and it wasn't just you making up your own mind. If we take decisions to Him with an open mind, He's not going to just sit and watch us make the wrong choice. He cares too much for us.

> The Spirit Himself testifies with our spirit that we are children of God. — (Romans 8:16)

God speaks to us most often through our spirit. Whether this is the witness of our spirit that tells us something is right or wrong, or whether it's something more, our spirit is hooked up to the Spirit of God. Start in the Word. As you begin to plant that word in your heart, you begin to recognize truth. This is one of those spots that defies a good explanation, but the best explanation I can give is to say there is a feel to truth. I've heard that the "witness of the Spirit" is the Holy Spirit telling our spirit that something is good or bad. I suspect as you have truth revealed to you in the Bible, you begin to recognize that feeling. The feeling of God bringing to life truth into you. Then, when you're listening to a message or reading a book, you can get that same feel. It's like the Holy Spirit is saying "Yes! Yes!" inside of you. To me, that's the next step in hearing from the Spirit. That basic feel of right vs wrong. It's a guide for us as we navigate this life.

As you continue, you begin learning to recognize His voice. In physical terms, it's like hearing the inflections in the voice and the way someone talks. You can pick them out just from how their voice sounds. In spiritual terms it's more like an undeniable truth and the emotion that it comes across with. God can and may speak externally to you. From my understanding God will work that way when He must, but tends to speak internally to us, Spirit to spirit. Why? I don't know. But if you look around you and listen to those who know His voice, this is what you'll find. If you are wondering how God sounds when He speaks to you, He sounds just like you. For example, have you ever thought that you heard your name said, but decided it must have just been in your imagination? Or have you ever been thinking one train of thought and suddenly have a very clear and distinct thought (often words) come into your mind about a different topic. Many of these incidents are thoughts coming from the spiritual realm. Notice that I didn't say the Holy Spirit, because God isn't the only one trying to get our attention. I have had plenty of thoughts pop into my mind telling me to do something I shouldn't that are very clearly not of God. This was the enemy trying to entice me into sin.

The hard part is discerning the source of the communication. Often the motive can give it away. For example, have you ever suddenly had the urge to just call a friend and encourage them? Or have you had an overwhelming desire to stop and give money to someone. In these cases, you can tell that compassion or love is behind the thought. Sometimes I can just feel a certain emotion or character to the words. Is it calm and dignified, or rash and abrasive? Helpful or hurtful? Ask the Holy Spirit to help here, as that's one of the things He has come for. Does the voice have the same feel as the

Lord? Try to recognize when He's speaking to you and act upon it. It takes time. You can't expect any part of it to go quickly unless God does so for a reason, but He wants us to grow in Him in this way.

If you want to learn His voice, you must spend quality time with Him. When you're taking some quiet time with the Lord, and you get a phone call, what do you do? Do you pick up the call and handle it or do you ignore it, knowing you can call them back later. Don't take the leftovers of the day and give it to him. This timing depends upon you. Some people have better times of the day. My test is whether I can focus and give Him undivided attention. There is no substitute for your time. Those who learn His voice have put in the time with Him. I am not saying you need huge amounts of time to stay quiet in your closet with God, though that's probably still one of the best ways. You give Him the time you can. Quiet times are great, but so are continued discussions during the day, talking while driving, and meditating while mowing. Fill your mind with God.

When We've Lost His Voice

Perhaps you've felt like you have had times in the past where the Lord is speaking, but have since gone quiet. You pray, but don't seem to get anything anymore. Is it something wrong you have done? It's possible, but if that is the case, then you probably know it already. What do you do when you get to this point? When you can't seem to hear what God's telling you to do? Start with what you know. Go back to the last thing you felt He said, and start there. Maybe you still haven't finished with that lesson and you're not ready for the next. Also keep in mind, God's priorities are not our priorities. How often did Jesus answer people in a way that seemed confusing? His heart was on the kingdom—His thoughts more in the spirit than in the flesh—so many of His answers didn't make as much sense at the time for those who are tuned into the flesh. Trust in the Lord and what He's led you to.

Moving Past Words

> Blessed are the pure in heart, for they shall see God.
> — (Matthew 5:8)

Surely we can't see God, right? Verses like this we tend to spiritualize as our experience tells us it isn't so. Does this actually speak of seeing the Lord face to face, seeing Him in our spirit as in a dream, or seeing the effect of Him upon our surroundings through ourselves and others? We know God is moving, so to see Him is perhaps to recognize where He is working. Yet, I believe it's more. My spirit says that if the Bible says this, it's possible. I've always longed to see more of God. Scripture backs me up.

> After a little while the world will no longer see Me, but you will see Me; because I live, you will live also.
> — (John 14:19)

The world won't see Jesus, but the disciples still will.

> For the Lord is righteous, He loves righteousness; the upright will behold His face. — (Psalm 11:7)

I know this could sound weird, but I want to see the Lord. Some people might want to throw me into a strange religious group with that comment, but my response is "why would I not desire this?" I think it's perfectly normal. You see, I love Him. I worship Him, I rely upon Him, and I talk with Him. He is my Father and what child cannot see his family? What do you call that sort of relationship here on earth where a child cannot see their family? Why would I not want to see them around me as well? I have always felt that my shortcomings are what is keeping me from seeing more of the heavenly realm, which lines up with the verse above about the pure in heart. I began believing that my holiness is part of what will draw me closer to Him, and allow me a more open view. Then one day I found this verse.

> Pursue peace with all men, and the sanctification without which no one will see the Lord. — (Hebrews 12:14)

Guess that settles it. As we clear up the clutter in our lives, we open our eyes. As God's grace gives us victory over our sins, we become more like Jesus. As this process continues, we grow up in godliness, and begin to know the Lord. Just as we learn to hear His voice, we can learn to recognize His presence and involvement around us. We see Him moving through people, for we've seen Him do the same in ourselves. We can see even more. Just look to the Bible and see all the dreams, visions, angels and other things that occurred to the saints. God doesn't change.

Be With Him

Now go be with Him. Don't spend all day living your life and then come to Him at the end for a little quiet time. Invite Him into your life. Do things with the Lord, whether this be your work, driving, reading, or even eating. Always remember, God is a person. So just as you would a spouse, parent, or child; be involved with Him. Don't fill your mind with music every spare moment, but open it up to conversation. When you're working, discuss your problems with Him. When you find some quiet time, come to Him in prayer and study His word. When you eat, do it in thankfulness of the blessings He's provided. When you speak with others, brag on Him like you would your spouse if they were with you.

Then trust Him. Trust that your Father who holds the world in His hand can lift you up in it as well. This doesn't mean something bad won't happen. Nor does it mean He will keep you from all evil. What it means is that He is with you. When trouble comes, you are not alone. And what's the worst that can happen? You go home to your beloved. This should inspire us all to overlook our earthly problems. What can our enemies do but drive us ever on toward the Lord. If we live, we become more like Him. If we die, we are with Him.

Kingdom Come

> Repent, for the kingdom of heaven is at hand. — (Matthew 3:2)

Imagine yourself in Israel during Jesus's day. You've been hearing about this man preaching in the wilderness all week. Most of the people just laugh and wave him off as crazy. You want to as well, yet you've seen how some people talk about him. The look in their eyes tell you there is something strange about this man out in the wilderness. Surely, he must be crazy. Dressed in camels' skins and living off the locusts. Of course, God wouldn't use a man like this. It's all just too absurd, yet each day you hear a little more until finally you have to go find out for yourself. After work, you leave town and follow the crowds out into the wilderness. There are no roads here, no shops or houses, just the brush. You nearly turn back several times wondering what in the world you're doing, but it's that curiosity which keeps you moving. At last you come to a river where the crowd has gathered and there he is, dirty, unkempt, and loud. He looks more like an outcast than a preacher. Yet his confidence and the tone of his voice tell you he believes deeply in what he says. The crowds just stare in awe. There's something in the air, something flowing through the crowd that says this is more than just a man yelling at a crowd. Something special is here. Your heart beats harder and there's a pressure in the air that excites you. You stop and listen to his words.

> Now in those days John the Baptist came, preaching in the wilderness of Judea, saying "Repent, for the kingdom of heaven is at hand" — (Matthew 3:1-2)

What is this kingdom of heaven? The Israelites were waiting for their messiah to set the nation free from their oppressors. Perhaps

John was speaking of the kingdom of Israel being resurrected? If that was the case, why would he baptize? I can imagine their confusion. Perhaps they came because they recognized the truth, but if so, it wasn't what they expected. He brought a change in heart, but more questions than answers. As time moves a little farther forward, we find Jesus coming into the scene after His temptation was done and beginning His ministry.

> From that time Jesus began to preach and say, "Repent, for the kingdom of heaven is at hand." — (Matthew 4:17)

Notice the similarity? The part that gets me curious is the message they preached. If God had asked me to go prepare the way for Jesus, what would I preach? I've gone to church for many years and read a lot of books about God. Surely I could come up with something to say. Here's the sort of messages I would've given:

- Repent, for the grace of God is coming
- Repent, forgiveness is at hand
- God is making a way for us
- Prepare to save yourself from hell

If I were to pick a message from my own understanding, my messages would speak of grace, heaven, and salvation. Perhaps I'd also speak of the peace of God coming. Instead, we find the focus of John and Jesus on the kingdom of heaven. Why the difference? Fairly often as believers we find our focus set differently than Jesus's. Look for yourself as you read the gospels; all it takes is a little time to consider His words. Jesus came to earth to preach the kingdom. Have you noticed how often the phrases "kingdom of God" and "kingdom of heaven" are used in the New Testament? Jesus spoke regarding the kingdom of God 130 times in the gospels. How often do you hear a sermon about the kingdom in church? In the churches I have been to, not too often. You hear messages about parts of the kingdom of course, but rarely about the kingdom itself. Do you feel the body of Christ is sharing the gospel of the kingdom or the gospel of grace? As followers of Christ, we need to be honest enough with ourselves to recognize that just because something is tradition, it doesn't make it right. Instead, we need to take what the Lord shows us and trust it.

> After his suffering, he showed himself to these men and gave many convincing proofs that he was alive. He appeared to them over a period of forty days and spoke about the kingdom of God. — (Acts 1:3)

How I wish I had those sermons recorded. Can you imagine; Jesus teaching about the kingdom to a group of disciples who have begun to see the picture. We need to understand that our lives are about much more than just forgiveness of our sins. We have been given more than that. How grieved God must be that we only take a part of what Jesus provided after He suffered so much to pay for it. The kingdom of God has come and Jesus has ushered it in. Until we understand more of the kingdom, we will not live up to the potential God has for His people. Need some proof? Let's look at John the Baptist. John had declared Jesus as the messiah the Israelites were waiting upon, but while he was in prison, he began having doubts. So, he sent his disciples to check.

> Summoning two of his disciples, John sent them to the Lord, saying, "Are You the Expected One, or do we look for someone else?" — (Luke 7:19)

Jesus responds.

> And He answered and said to them, "Go and report to John what you have seen and heard: the blind receive sight, the lame walk, the lepers are cleansed, and the deaf hear, the dead are raised up, the poor have the gospel preached to them. — (Luke 7:22)

What were the signs of the kingdom coming? People healed, lives restored, and the good news spread. The kingdom is not just a message of forgiveness, but of a grace and love which outpours unto changed lives. The actions of Jesus tell us that God is here and cares about us; not just the future us after death, but us right now. If we can accept it, these things can and do still happen today. Jesus has not changed, only we have.

Church Or Kingdom

The kingdom is greater than our churches today. I can see why many people on the outside look in and don't want what we have; as so many of us have become those Paul spoke against who were *"holding to a form of godliness, although they have denied its power"* (2 Timothy 3:5). We want our Bible studies and our church functions, but don't desire God ruling our lives. We judge our members by their participation in church activities and not their walk with the Lord. We've taken God's house of prayer and made it into a scout group with attendance and patches for accomplishments. We flaunt how much people give to shame others into doing their share. We push acting godly over being godly. We attempt to structure God, as if He's our servant.

That was perhaps a little harsh, but there are many truths in it that we need to understand. Don't get me wrong here; I love our churches. In most cases we are a genuine people sincerely reaching for our God. That doesn't mean we don't do silly or incorrect things. I have watched churches who seemed to praise their church more than their God. I've seen people bullied out of churches for their beliefs. I've seen people speak badly of that church across the street as if they are better. I've seen members shamed into giving for a building campaign. I've seen small groups shun members and Sunday school members gossip about those who don't fit. I've seen us count our attendance and compare our churches to show how great we are. We are a silly people that God has given much grace to.

Doctrines Of Man

Unfortunately, division has separated the kingdom. We're coming to a time where the kingdom will again take precedence over the church. One difference between the kingdom and the church is unity. The kingdom is unified under one King. The church has been fractured into so many denominations and doctrines, that we can't stand together. We bicker and fight about our beliefs, canons, and doctrines, but we forget one thing. There is only one King. When we split a church based on a difference in belief, both lose. You can tell the difference in a man by what he says. A church man talks about his church, denomination, and doctrines. A kingdom man talks about his King.

What I have found to be a stumbling block in our church is our need to build doctrines based upon our understanding rather than God's revelation. Not only do we try to place rules upon our brothers, we write them down and try to enforce them. We create creeds and doctrines that are easier for us to understand, rather than following the Spirit of God. We sprinkle or we immerse. We praise with instruments or we praise only with voices. We tithe or we give first fruits. We allow others into communion or just members. We baptize the saved simply because they're new to our denomination. We force signs to prove to others we are saved.

Our doctrines are wrong. Tell me this, when Jesus prayed His final prayer with the disciples, did He pray for church divisions? Did He ask for different denominations to stand in different areas and fight amongst themselves? No, He prayed for unity among believers. I am amazed at those who believe that their doctrine is correct. What they are believing is that out of the thousands of denominations, their specific choice has everything right? That's thinking a lot of themselves. I'm of the view that all our denominations have bits to offer. Some may be closer than others, but it's the full church that God wants; all the pieces of the body, not just some. Let's set aside our laws, our expectations, our doctrines, and our rules; and let's come together to find the Jesus we forgot that was the reason for it all.

> For our struggle is not against flesh and blood, but against the rulers, against the powers, against the world forces of this darkness, against the spiritual forces of wickedness in the heavenly places. — (Ephesians 6:12)

Who do we fight? Too often it is ourselves. Tough times come and we attack each other rather than rally together. In our struggles, we often forget who the real enemy is. The enemy is the spirit behind our problem, not the person who brings it. We suffer and turn our anger against another, as we find our troubles easier with someone to blame. When we work as part of the kingdom of God, our goal is united. We stand under the same King. Our focus should be upon that goal, and we should stand together against the enemy. When tough times come we should hold each other up, not tear each other down.

Unity Of The Body

The kingdom includes, loves, and understands. In the kingdom, we find it's all about the King. We can work together as a body rather than separately as churches. We're happy to send new believers to other churches because we can trust the Spirit to guide them rather than the church leaders. We invite people to find God rather than our church. We have no need to count our numbers for our confidence comes from pleasing Him. We do what we hear from high, rather than following what man tells us. We are members together who need each other, and God has given us all different gifts to help each other out. He's not going to give everything required to a single person, or what need would they have to work with others. If that did happen, they would begin to think they have all the answers. God spreads what is necessary among us all and we must work together to reach our full potential as His body. We're not made to be equal, but to become whole together

> I do not ask on behalf of these alone, but for those also who believe in Me through their word; that they may all be one; even as You, Father, are in Me and I in You, that they also may be in Us, so that the world may believe that You sent Me. The glory which You have given Me I have given to them, that they may be one, just as We are one; I in them and You in Me, that they may be perfected in unity, so that the world may know that You sent Me, and loved them, even as You have loved Me. — (John 17:20-23)

How many times did Jesus say "one" or "unity" in this passage? At the end of His ministry, He was concerned that His followers stay in union with each other and God. Looking at us now, I can see why. We are divided. We've lost unity with the Father, which has led to disunity among each other. Yet there is one Father and one truth.

> Therefore I, the prisoner of the Lord, implore you to walk in a manner worthy of the calling with which you have been called, with all humility and gentleness, with patience, showing tolerance for one another in love, being diligent to preserve the unity of the Spirit in the bond of peace. There is one body and one Spirit, just as also you were called in one hope of your calling; one Lord, one faith, one baptism, one God and Father of all who is over all and through all and in all. — (Ephesians 4:1-6)

As members of the kingdom of God, God is the father and we are all His children. We are together in this, which is why we call each other brothers and sisters in Christ. If you haven't noticed, God is big on family. Sometimes we overlook this. He instituted marriage. He created us to have children. One of the Ten Commandments He gave was to honor our parents. He even said in the last days that Elijah would come again to "restore the hearts of the fathers to their children and the hearts of the children to their fathers" (Malachi 4:6). How then can we recognize who is our family?

> For whoever does the will of My Father who is in heaven, he is My brother and sister and mother. — (Matthew 12:50)

This is a kingdom point of view we must find. We can all look up to our King and follow His commands, but we aren't all to know everything that is going on. Others in the kingdom will do things we cannot understand, because they work in a different area and have a different mission. We must have a loyalty to our King that leads us to do our part no matter what others do. We do the work we've been given. When you hear about the success of others, rejoice. Do not struggle and compete. If a brother gets a break-through, rejoice with him and do not envy. God has chosen to use us all. Our brother's or sister's victory is also our victory. Jesus prayed much for unity; let us not forget this.

Not Far From The Kingdom

Now let's discuss what the kingdom is. The first question we will start with is: where is the kingdom? We could say that the kingdom is in heaven, that it is on earth, or that it's just a "spiritual" concept to represent God's people. We'll find our first clue in Jesus's model prayer.

> Your kingdom come your will be done, on earth as it is in heaven. — (Matthew 6:10)

Jesus makes it clear that the kingdom is not just in heaven. Sometimes we want to think of the kingdom as "spiritual" only, that we just need to hold onto our faith until the end of our lives and we'll reach the kingdom; however, that is not how Jesus told us to pray. Jesus prayed that God's kingdom would come on earth, as it is in heaven. Jesus was directing us to pray for God to bring more of His kingdom to the earth. I am certain some will interpret this last verse in a way to say the kingdom has yet to come to earth and won't until the second coming. If you're considering this, the next passage will clear that up.

> Now having been questioned by the Pharisees as to when the kingdom of God was coming, He answered them and said, "The kingdom of God is not coming with signs to be observed; nor will they say, 'Look, here it is!' or, 'There it is!' For behold, the kingdom of God is in your midst." — (Luke 17:20–21)

If I'm to be honest, I'm not sure if the kingdom existed upon the earth before Jesus. That's a bit outside of my level of revelation; however, I know it was here while Jesus walked the earth and has continued since. The way I look at it, Jesus ushered the kingdom into our world. He brought it for us to see and touch; His life and death paving a way for the kingdom to enter our very lives. You see, the kingdom is here, it is now, and it is among us.

> Jesus answered, "My kingdom is not of this world. If My kingdom were of this world, then My servants would be fighting so that I would not be handed over to the Jews; but as it is, My kingdom is not of this realm." — (John 18:36)

Not only is the kingdom here, but it's also not from this world. That means it is not a church, a section of land, or even a certain set of people; the kingdom is much more. Too often we treat the kingdom as a physical thing. It's the number of people in our congregation, the size of our budget, or the number of baptisms we've had this year. We act too much like old Israel, who wanted to count their numbers. They would stand against an opponent and fear when they were outnumbered, forgetting that with God the physical reality of the world was never an issue. He would rout an army by a word from His mouth.

> For He rescued us from the domain of darkness, and transferred us to the kingdom of His beloved Son. — (Colossians 1:13)

What began with God in heaven has come to the earth. We were brought into this kingdom through the blood of Jesus alone. God has never been concerned with what we can provide, but rather with what we will give up for Him. We stand for the name of our King, not for any human group. We are not only a part of this kingdom, but also ambassadors of it.

It is not about what we do, but who we are dwelling in. In essence, the kingdom is the realm of God. If you were to think about an earthly kingdom, then where does that kingdom reach? It reaches to everywhere that is ruled by the king. This does not include all the things you may think. Just because we call ourselves a church doesn't means we're a part of the kingdom. This earth is not currently His realm. I know that may sound odd, but if you look in scripture you'll find that God gave authority over earth to man all the way back with Adam. Adam then handed that over to Satan up until Jesus came and began the process of freeing the world. The act of bringing the kingdom to earth means we must bring ourselves into submission to the King. As we do this, we display the very nature of God, showing His power, glory, and attributes to this world. As we bring our lives into submission with Him, our lives will become a part of the kingdom and the world around us will change. For His own reasons, God has given the authority back to us. The world will not change without us involved.

Foolish Things

I know much of this is abstract, and it can be difficult to understand. Unfortunately, I can only do so much here. The wisdom of God is not the understanding of man. We must come to understand God's ways and receive revelation from Him to begin understanding the kingdom. For the things of God will not make sense to this world. In one of Jesus's prayers He says these words:

> I praise You, Father, Lord of heaven and earth, that You have hidden these things from the wise and intelligent and have revealed them to infants. — (Luke 10:21)

Paul describes this in different words in his letter to the Corinthians.

> But God has chosen the foolish things of the world to shame the wise, and God has chosen the weak things of the world to shame the things which are strong. — (1 Corinthians 1:27)

God's wisdom is not ours. Strangely, this is one of those things we all know, and yet we all tend to forget. Why? Because we rely upon our own wisdom to make choices. We minister from our strength. We debate with only our intellect. There's a difference in ministering from our minds and from the power of God. God's wisdom is different than our intelligence. I am continually reminded as I watch Christians trying to convince people of the truth by their own intellect. We argue and attempt to persuade, but do so by using our own words and understanding. We quote our theologians and authors as if their titles add validity to the lost. Honestly, the world doesn't care. The only way to reach them is through truth from God. We should learn to receive from the kingdom itself and show that to the world, not our understanding.

Entering The Kingdom

> But when the king came in to look over the dinner guests, he saw a man there who was not dressed in wedding clothes, and he said to him, "Friend, how did you come in here without wedding clothes?" And the man was speechless. Then the king said to the servants, "Bind him hand and foot, and throw him into the outer darkness; in that place there will be weeping and gnashing of teeth." For many are called, but few are chosen. — (Matthew 22:11–14)

God has sent out His invitation to all. We are told that God is "not wishing for any to perish but for all to come to repentance" (2 Peter 3:9). However, only those who accept it, who buy from the Lord "white garments so that you may clothe yourself" (Revelation 3:18), will be accepted. Whenever you see white in the Bible, you can generally think righteousness and purity. These clothes are the righteousness we find in Jesus. The garments of grace that cover over our sin are required for us to enter into the kingdom.

> Truly I say to you, whoever does not receive the kingdom of God like a child will not enter it at all. — (Luke 18:17)

We come as a child. Coming into the kingdom is not something that we can understand or do ourselves. What's so special about a child? They will trust implicitly and express absolutely. If their parent tells them something, they just believe. They don't need explanations; it is enough that their parents know. They are open and honest, as they haven't learned to put on the masks we wear. Only as we come before the King with humility and openness, can the kingdom even be revealed to us. I'll speak in more depth on this later, but humility before God is one of the biggest keys to moving forward in Him.

Until we can let go of what we think we know, willingly accepting Him for who He is and ourselves as we are, we can only grow so far.

> Jesus answered and said to him, "Truly, truly, I say to you, unless one is born again he cannot see the kingdom of God." — (John 3:3)

The entrance begins with salvation. Notice however that this verse doesn't say the those born again enter, but that those who are born again can see. Only once we are saved are we open to the possibility of seeing it at work and joining in.

> Jesus answered to them, "To you it has been granted to know the mysteries of the kingdom of heaven, but to them it has not been granted. For whoever has, to him more shall be given, and he will have an abundance; but whoever does not have, even what he has shall be taken away from him. Therefore I speak to them in parables, because while seeing they do not see, and while hearing they do not hear, nor do they understand." — (Matthew 13:11–13)

God granted understanding to the disciples. He allowed them to see the secrets of the kingdom, however the rest were not allowed to understand. Remember from the previous chapter that truth from God comes through revelation, we cannot find it ourselves. This is how salvation works. God reveals to us the truth and we can choose to accept it or not. He has to open our eyes to see and our ears to hear.

Revelations Of The Kingdom

As the kingdom is revealed to mankind, we find new revelations on top of the Old Testament beliefs.

The Nature of God

In Jesus last moments with His disciples in the garden before being led away, we find this prayer which He prayed over them.

> Father, the hour has come...
>
> That to all whom You have given Him, He may give eternal life...
>
> Now, Father, glorify Me together with Yourself..
>
> I have manifested Your name to the men whom you gave me...
>
> Holy Father, keep them in Your name..
>
> That they may all be one; even as You, Father, are in me and I in You...
>
> O righteous Father, although the world has not known You, yet I have known You; and these have known that You sent Me; and I have made Your name known to them, and will make it known, so that the love with which You loved Me may be in them, and I in them. — (John 17:1,2,6,11,21,25–26)

Given this prayer, what did Jesus come to do? He came to give us eternal life and something else. He came to make God's name known and to reveal His nature to us. There are many names given for God yet I only recall one name which Jesus regularly used. The one we just read many times in that prayer.

Father.

Never before was God referred to as Father. Jesus revealed to mankind a new aspect of God. Names in the Bible are significant as revealing the character of the person as well. Abraham had his name changed when God blessed him and Sarah, giving them the promise of El Shaddai. So, when Jesus revealed the Father to us, He was revealing the nature of God as well. Through His death, we are brought into the family of God.

> For all who are being led by the Spirit of God, these are sons of God. For you have not received a spirit of slavery leading to fear again, but you have received a spirit of adoption as sons, by which we cry out, "Abba! Father!" — (Romans 8:14-15)

The kingdom of God is about family. We are called by His name. We are known under our family name. Jesus came to reveal to us that we have been adopted into God, and that He is our Father. This is such a great revelation, and yet we overlook it. Christianity is unique in that God does not desire our acts but a relationship with us. This is the wonder of our God, that He wants to be a Father and enjoy a close relationship with us; not sit in heaven with a rulebook and a measuring stick.

Children of God

> You are from God, little children. — (1 John 4:4)

We are children of God. We have been brought into His family and given His name. As James says:

> Listen, my beloved brethren: did not God choose the poor of this world to be rich in faith and heirs of the kingdom which He promised to those who love Him? — (James 2:5)

God chose us. He brought us in and adopted us. As children, we are heirs of His kingdom. We can be given an authority that goes with this, as we have an inheritance and a King who is backing us.

Too often we look at our position and don't think much of ourselves, but that's not how God sees us. For example, let's take John the Baptist. As one of the greatest prophets, he was sent to prepare for the coming of Jesus. I would consider him one of the greatest men in the Bible, yet listen to Jesus's words.

> I say to you, among those born of women there is no one greater than John; yet he who is least in the kingdom of God is greater than he. — (Luke 7:28)

This truth always threw me for a loop. I would try to explain it away using salvation. We have more than John had at the time, but that can't explain why we are greater than Him. Our entrance into the kingdom has elevated us. Think about it, we have inside us the ability to be greater than John the Baptist even though we don't act like it. We don't have the confidence that we should as part of the kingdom.

> Truly, truly, I say to you, he who believes in Me, the works that I do, he will do also; and greater [works] than these he will do; because I go to the Father. — (John 14:12)

Tell me, are you doing greater work than Jesus? Why not? According to this verse, all it takes is for us to believe. Unfortunately, we trust our experience more than God's word. As children, we have access to an inheritance. We can grow into heirs with authority. It's not about you, rather it's about the God who works in you.

Immanuel
One of my favorite names for God in the Bible is Immanuel. It is only mentioned three times in the Bible, yet it speaks deeply to me. This was the name given for Jesus's entrance into this world. It simply means, "God with us".

> Behold, the virgin shall be with child and shall bear a son, and they shall call His name Immanuel", which translated means, "God with us." — (Matthew 1:23)

God had come as a pillar of fire and cloud before Moses and Israel. When Solomon dedicated the temple, the presence of God came like smoke. He thundered from the mountain, burned in the sky, and even lit up David's tabernacle. God manifested Himself many times to His people in such awe-inspiring ways; but not since Adam and Eve in the garden had we seen Him consistently walk among us until the coming of Jesus. Suddenly, it all changed. I love what that means for how much God loves us. Imagine how He could set aside His splendor to become a baby. Even more, this presence did not end with His death, for He sent another to us—the Holy Spirit. We have such a gift in a God this willing to share and be with us.

The Great Mystery

There is one more revelation even greater than the previous ones I've mentioned. It's a mystery more powerful than having God with us, more wonderful than God as our Father. It is the fulfillment of what the prophets of the Old Testament saw only at a distance. Paul spoke of it in Romans.

> Now to Him who is able to establish you according to my gospel and the preaching of Jesus Christ, according to the revelation of the mystery which has been kept secret for long ages past. — (Romans 16:25)

A mystery was revealed to the apostles; something that was to help establish the church.

> Of this church I was made a minister according to the stewardship from God bestowed on me for your benefit, so that I might fully carry out the preaching

> of the word of God, that is, the mystery which has been hidden from the past ages and generations, but has now been manifested to His saints, to whom God willed to make known what is the riches of the glory of this mystery among the Gentiles, which is Christ in you, the hope of glory. — (Colossians 1:25–27)

Christ in you. Not only do we have Immanuel, the God with us, we also can have Christ in us. Jesus can take up shop in our heart and walk with us. I'm not talking about the empty words we quote about Jesus living in us because we are saved. Salvation is just a step. It's the beginning of all the steps, but just a step. I'm speaking of more than this. Notice how Paul continues in his letter to the Colossians:

> That their hearts may be encouraged, having been knit together in love, and attaining to all the wealth that comes from the full assurance of understanding, resulting in a true knowledge of God's mystery, that is, Christ Himself, in whom are hidden all the treasures of wisdom and knowledge. — (Colossians 2:2–3)

Can you tell me that this is how you live, in "full assurance" and "true knowledge"? In this we find "all the treasure of wisdom and knowledge." This isn't your casual Christianity. This is not what you find in the person who shows up to church on Sunday and lives his own life the rest of the week. This is a transformed life. Come to think of it, this isn't a transformed life as much as another life lived out from you. This is not the type of life that just makes you nice and generous. This is the sort of life that when lived changes the world. This is a kingdom life.

My Yoke is Easy

> Come to Me, all who are weary and heavy-laden, and I will give you rest. Take My yoke upon you and learn from Me, for I am gentle and humble in heart, and you will find rest for your souls. For My yoke is easy and My burden is light. — (Matthew 11:28–30)

Would you describe Jesus's life as easy? Which periods of His ministry would you describe as light? Perhaps it was when He gave up such glory to put on flesh and become a helpless baby? Maybe when He was mocked by the world? How about when His own family didn't believe Him? Let's not forget when He was nearly stoned or when He was tempted for 40 days in the wilderness without food or drink? Let's not forget when He was beaten, stripped, whipped, ridiculed, and then crucified. His life looked rather difficult to me. I don't think anyone will disagree that especially after Jesus began His ministry, things were tough. He dealt with so many physical, emotional, and spiritual demands. Yet, what Jesus saw in this world and what we see are two different realities. We often find it hard to understand many of Jesus's teachings and parables because of this difference in perception. Jesus looked at this world and saw the spirit as truth, rendering His perception of the physical world formed through that lens. Jesus's truths were spiritual truths that superseded the physical. For example, take the woman at the well. The disciples asked Jesus if He was hungry because He hadn't eaten all day. His reply was that His food was to do the Father's will. His answer was spirit, and the spirit overrides the physical. Too often we take this physical world with what we see and try to make the spiritual truths match what we can perceive. This mistake can lead us away from the truth.

I look at Jesus's life and think about how physically demanding it was, which is my first mistake. When Jesus said "all who labor and are heavy laden," He was talking about our souls rather than our physical bodies. Our lives are hard because we put burdens upon ourselves that we weren't meant to bear. The worst of these can be the very religion we create. We put rules upon ourselves that must be followed and our own expectations wear us out. We attempt to please everyone and to fulfill every obligation. When we inevitably fail, that burdens us all the more. Look around and you can see it. So many Christians have run themselves ragged with their Christian lives. We are tired, beaten down, and struggling to keep afloat after attempting to keep up with our lives. We put such high expectations on ourselves that we can't help but fail. We feel like we must do so much, when so little is required.

Troubled By What We Believe

> Do not let your heart be troubled; believe in God, believe also in Me. — (John 14:1)

We read the Bible too quickly and miss the obvious. In this verse, Jesus is telling people to not let themselves be so troubled, and then gives them the alternative. If He tells you not to do something, then gives you an action; it's the solution. What did Jesus say was the cure for troubles? Believing in God. When we're troubled because we feel alone and helpless, believe in God. We make our lives overly complicated, but much of it comes back to the same principles. When Jesus was asked what the most important laws were, He told the questioner to love God and love his neighbors. We, however, see fit to add in our daily quiet times, our measured and planned-out prayers, our blessings for food, our thank you notes, our shower gifts, our Christmas stockings, our to-do lists, and so much more.

> No one can serve two masters; for either he will hate the one and love the other, or he will be devoted to

one and despise the other, you cannot serve God and wealth. — (Matthew 6:24)

We find ourselves in trouble as we try to please too many people. We say that we want to please God, but then we find ourselves constantly watching our bank account. We desire the latest device, clothing, or car. We buy big houses, fancy cars, and little crosses to hang in them. We try so hard to make our family happy by providing for and pleasing them, and then wonder why we can't seem to make it work. We want to please the Lord, but spend so much on ourselves that we leave little for Jesus. Anything that is not an extension of our devotion to the Lord can cause us to split our focus. When the two don't align, we must fight harder to hold onto both. The only answer is the death of all other passions before the Lord.

For what I am doing, I do not understand; for I am not practicing what I would like to do, but I am doing the very thing I hate. — (Romans 7:15)

These words have been interpreted many ways, but however you look at it, Paul was speaking of the trouble from trying to do the right things. We know what is right, but we can't seem to pull it all off. We find that the more we understand and want the good, the farther away we seem to be. Yet, I love how Paul ends this chapter.

Thanks be to God through Jesus Christ our Lord! — (Romans 7:25)

We are inadequate; we can only find that peace through our Lord Jesus.

What Did Jesus Come To Do

How did Jesus handle this? We can see what Jesus said that He did on this earth.

> Therefore Jesus answered and was saying to them, 'Truly, truly, I say to you, the Son can do nothing of Himself, unless it is something He sees the Father doing; for whatever the Father does, these things the Son also does in like manner." — (John 5:19)

When Jesus needed to choose what to do, He would look to the Father. If it's something the Father was doing, then it was good for Jesus to do. He knew if He pleased the Father, that was all that's required. Most of us don't have the Father in such close relationship as Jesus, but we can use what we have. The first thing we have is Jesus. We have His words and His actions written in the Bible. Jesus didn't come to place more rules and requirements, but to free us from them. We're now under love, not rules. The Christian life seems hard when we attempt to love other things more than God. Things become difficult when we walk a tightrope between two worlds. Imagine a man trying to date two women. In the end, he'll lose both. Jesus spoke on this at the Sermon on the Mount. We cannot serve two masters. Instead Jesus gave us the gospel.

> And with your feet fitted with the readiness that comes from the gospel of peace. — (Ephesians 6:15)

Jesus's gospel is the gospel of peace. He's come to bring us peace. This is not only a peace between God and us, but also a peace in our own hearts. No longer do we need to worry about all the worldly things that affect us. We put on our feet the gospel of peace. Everywhere we go, we walk in this. This isn't the gospel of salvation, though salvation is part of the message. This isn't a gospel of love, though God loves us so much. It's a gospel of peace. We can have a peace in what the Lord has done for us, what He is doing for us, and what He has set before us.

And My Burden Is Light

How was it that Jesus's burden could be light? Because out of love, He surrendered to the Father's will and did what the Father led Him to do. The burden to save the world was not on Jesus; He only had to do what He saw the Father doing. The burden was upon God. God has created our lives and set a path before us. It is for Him to work everything out, we need only to rely upon Him. Cast your cares upon Him.

> For this is the love of God, that we keep His commandments; and His commandments are not burdensome. For whatever is born of God overcomes the world; and this is the victory that has overcome the world — our faith. — (1 John 5:3)

His commandments aren't burdensome, which means the burdens we carry so heavily are the ones we've placed upon ourselves. Following God will be demanding, but it will not burden you down. There's an important distinction there. Think of it as the difference between the body and the soul. Our body can quickly recover from being burdened down. We feel sore for a few days, stretch the muscles, and feel better. Our soul doesn't seem to recover so quickly. Burdens upon our soul weigh us down more than weights on our body ever will. You will find as you give more to God, things become easier. You will worry less, because you trust God more and know that your actions are not in vain.

Do Not Worry

> Be anxious for nothing, but in everything by prayer and supplication with thanksgiving let your requests be made known to God. And the peace of God which surpasses all comprehension, shall guard your hearts and your minds in Christ Jesus. — (Philippians 4:6-7)

We must learn to not be anxious. We have all heard verses that speak about God watching out for us and not being separated from His love. Even so, few of us walk like that. Stop worrying so much. After we had our child, my wife and I suddenly found ourselves not only in the position of raising a baby, but also building a house and trying to sell our current home all at the same time. Let me start by saying that I don't recommend this. Still, we ended up here through this strange combination of circumstances and through a belief that God was with us. Then we sat with a "For Sale" sign in our yards for months. We had some lookers, but no bites. The longer we went, the more nervous we became. This is when anxiety reared its ugly head. We had to take the time to consider our options, look at the price, do open houses, and work on a budget for the possible outcome. The problem is that all I wanted to do was worry about this. I would go over numbers in my head, trying to work through our budget and finances over and over. I found out there is a point where prudence gives way to anxiety. When I reached that point, I had to make the best decision I could and move on. The enemy kept pouring thoughts of worry, fear, and over-planning into my head. These thoughts would then push out the more important aspects of my life. I often caught myself during a quiet time with the Lord thinking about what price to put on the house rather than His greatness. Peter says it very simply:

> Cast all your anxiety on Him, because He cares for you. — (1 Peter 5:7)

We have attempted to justify our anxiety by calling it responsibility. Because we do not trust that God cares for us, we've created a belief around our doubts and tried to paint it as being good stewards. What I came to realize is that God wasn't nearly as worried about me losing money on that house as I was. He had plenty. Instead, as Philippians 4 states, I needed to learn to let peace guard my heart. We speak of peace as something to make us happy, but not as the root of our walk. Jesus is the Prince of Peace. We should not marginalize peace.

It will protect our heart from many of the snares of the devil. Keep in mind this proverb:

> Above all else, guard your heart, for everything you do flows from it. — (Proverbs 4:23)

The Lord has continued to bring me back to this over and over; to keep my heart upon what was important and not upon the worries of finances. When I returned to the Lord asking if this was His will or if I made a mistake, I wouldn't get an answer. After some time, I realized that was purposeful. If God needed to answer my doubts every time an issue popped up, then my faith wasn't going to grow. Even more, let's pretend that I really did make a bad choice and this is going to come back to cause me a lot of financial issues. So what. What do I really need in place of a God who showers me with inconceivable love? What if we lost our house? What if I had to sacrifice our middle-class lifestyle? Would my life be worse for this? Or could I, like Paul, find contentment in any circumstance, for Jesus is there in them all?

> For this reason I say to you, do not be worried about your life, as to what you will eat or what you will drink; nor for your body, as to what you will put on. Is not life more than food, and the body more than clothing? ... But seek first His kingdom and His righteousness, and all these things will be added to you. — (Matthew 6:25,33)

We don't ignore the world, but we also don't focus upon it. In every situation we bring our needs to the Lord and we focus upon Him. Commit yourself to prayer and God's peace will guard you. Often, we try to control everything, feeling like it must all go correctly or we will fail. Let me tell you a secret. You are not in control. You cannot control friends, family, spouse, or even your possessions. There's only one thing you can control and that is your actions. For this reason, don't fret everything else. Just make sure your response counts. That's all you can do anyway. Put your faith in the Lord, and find His peace. You know you found real peace when it is at odds with what the world says. When logic says you should be afraid and yet you feel calm. Hold onto that. Stay in the Lord and let His peace guard your heart.

Let's read through Psalm 23, looking at how David walked.

> The Lord is my shepherd, I shall not want.
> He makes me lie down in green pastures;
> He leads me beside quiet waters.
> He restores my soul;
> He guides me in the paths of righteousness For His name's sake.
> Even though I walk through the valley of the shadow of death, I fear no evil, for You are with me;
> Your rod and Your staff, they comfort me.
> You prepare a table before me in the presence of my enemies;
> You have anointed my head with oil;
> My cup overflows.
> Surely goodness and lovingkindness will follow me all the days of my life,
> And I will dwell in the house of the Lord forever.

These words were written by a man who had Saul hunting him for years trying to kill him, only to lose his best friend in the moment he found freedom. He had not one, but two sons attempt to crown themselves king without his consent. One of them ran him into hiding before he was overthrown. He had another son die for his(David's) sins with Bathsheba. He was constantly at war with his neighbors. David learned these truths as a shepherd. He followed God as his sheep must have followed him; knowing that his shepherd will know the way to food, water, and shelter. David knew his shepherd would give him contentment, for sheep need peace more than any other herded creatures. They are easily afraid and quickly lose health when they are not provided a safe place to rest. Among the wars, the flights, and the deaths; David found the peace that God provides for those who are devoted to Him.

One point I want to make here. Just because you are saved, that doesn't mean God will protect you from everything. Too often I hear these canned responses from people saying God will take care of everything, but I worry if those people are trusting upon God to lead or just blindly believing it will all work out. A sheep can walk off the cliff while believing the shepherd will protect him all the way down to his death. No, the sheep must stay near the shepherd and follow his commands. The sheep must be devoted only to the shepherd. This is where we fall away. We like our own things and follow our own advice. We haven't taken that step into bond-service that is required. Another famous Psalm that speaks about God watching over us is Psalm 91. It begins with this verse.

> He who dwells in the shelter of the Most High
> Will abide in the shadow of the Almighty. — (Psalm 91:1)

Psalm 91 has many promises of protection for its audience, yet we mustn't forget where it begins. The King James version says, "He who dwells in the secret place of the Most High". Can you honestly say that you feel like you're in the secret place of God, or do you just show up to church and do the requirements laid before you? Why should you expect the promises if you're not doing the action the passage requires of you? If you want the comfort of the shepherd, you must follow him. Stand firm in the Lord. Isaiah tells us:

> The steadfast of mind You will keep in perfect peace,
> because he trusts in You. — (Isaiah 26:3–4)

Trust in the Lord. As you continue to do this, standing among the problems this world will throw at you, you will find yourself upon a rock. The problems make get bigger with life, but you will continually find your God even larger than you thought. Worship the

Lord with your life. Bring your thoughts to Him whenever you can. Praise Him in all circumstances. As your focus moves to Him and away from yourself, peace will flow over you. You can give thanks to God even in the troubles, for they will only make you stronger if you trust in the Lord.

> Let the peace of God rule your heart — (Colossians 3:15)

Peace isn't something you act out, nor can you wear it like clothing. No, peace must rule your life.

PART 2 — THE FOUNDATIONS

Therefore leaving the elementary teaching about the Christ, let us press on to maturity, not laying again a foundation of repentance from dead works and of faith toward God, of instruction about washings and laying on of hands, and the resurrection of the dead and eternal judgment.

— (Hebrews 6:1–2)

Grace To Live

> But if the ministry of death, in letters engraved on stones, came with glory, so that the sons of Israel could not look intently at the face of Moses because of the glory of his face, fading as it was, how will the ministry of the Spirit fail to be even more with glory? For if the ministry of condemnation has glory, much more does the ministry of righteousness abound in glory. — (2 Corinthians 3:7–9)

For the most part, the church has taken the Old Testament Law and placed it aside as something wholly unnecessary. We believe it has little relevance to our lives under Jesus, and our knowledge of the law shows the truth of it. Even given this, as I came across this verse I was surprised to find the Law labelled as the "ministry of death". Hard words to describe the law which proceeded from the mouth of God. Yet, God did not bring the Law to save us, for we can never live up to it. The Law is so perfect, that we could never hope to be righteous. This was God's plan all along. We needed to see a little glimpse of what holiness looks like in man. God used the law to show us our shortcomings and to lead us to the point where we cry for mercy to Him.

God desired to keep Man from falling too far away. Starting with the sin of Adam, mankind progressed farther and farther into darkness until there were only a few left that God could work with. Then, like a surgeon cutting away the gangrene, God sent the flood to wipe away that which couldn't be saved. The declined continued. Next, God gave the Law to Moses. As mankind continued to turn away from God and not seek his mercy, God needed to make it clear how wicked man was. The Law was laid out telling the Israelites what was good and what was bad. It made lists of foods that could be eaten, and those that couldn't. It listed items that could be touched, and those that couldn't. It told them what was clean and what wasn't. It gave descriptions of how to wash, what to wear, and when to work. It spoke of priests, rules, and sacrifices. The Law laid it all out and drew a line. Over here is good; over there is bad. If you haven't read all the way through Leviticus, just trust me that it was very detailed. God set a bar for man that no one could ever reach.

Then they tried. They would attempt to follow for a while, then fall away. They would keep the Law they were comfortable with and leave out the rest. They even made up new rules on top of the Law. In the end, it all failed. The Law could not justify man. Under the Law, Israel gave sacrifices for their sins. The Law taught that man would sin and atonement must be made. Blood sacrifices were given to cover over our sin. But the Law was not the answer, as the Law could not overcome sin. It could help keep man from falling too far into sin, and cover it for a time, but it could not save man. Paul said in it this way in Galatians:

> Nevertheless knowing that a man is not justified by the works of the Law but through faith in Christ Jesus, even we have believed in Christ Jesus, so that we may be justified by faith in Christ and not by the works of the Law; since by the works of the Law no flesh will be justified. — (Galatians 2:16)

Law Alone Leads To Religion

When you create a set of rules and focus too much upon them rather than the purpose behind them, it turns into a religion that isn't that much different than all the others. For example, when the Pharisees attempted to judge Jesus by their rules, He quoted Hosea to them.

> But go and learn what this means: 'I desire compassion, and not sacrifice,' for I did not come to call the righteous, but sinners. — (Matthew 9:13)

Israel fell into religion, trying to follow the Law but forgetting the God behind it. They put their trust into the sacrifices and burnt offerings. Rather, according to David in Psalm 51, the sacrifices of God are "a broken spirit, a broken and contrite heart." God desires brokenness and humility, not adherence toward rules. When you break it down, religion is man's attempt to reach God by following a set of rules to make themselves righteous. I still don't understand what our fascination seems to be with following religion rather than building a relationship. We have a God that has saved us, but we feel more comfortable when we make up our own version of what God wants from us and what we need to do.

The religious people were one of the few that Jesus openly rebuked in His time in the world. He was gracious towards the tax-collectors, prostitutes, and sinners, but condemning to those who tried to act self-righteously. Jesus loves an open heart, even from those who are in the depths of sin, but He turns away those who have built themselves upon their works.

> Behold I, Paul, say to you that if you receive circumcision, Christ will be of no benefit to you. And I testify again to every man who receives circumcision, that he is under obligation to keep the whole Law... For in Christ Jesus neither circumcision nor uncircumcision means anything, but faith working through love. — (Galatians 5:2–3,6)

Religion can be so much easier than relationship. It's simpler to follow a rule than it is to stay in communion. I've heard it said, "We want to serve a God that we won't take the time to get to know". We find ourselves doing what we think is right, instead of humbling ourselves to learn what God really wants of us. Stay in a church for a while and there's a good chance you'll see this. People sincerely want to know God's will for their lives. They go to church, do their jobs, take care of their families, and try to be good, but still worry that maybe they should be doing more. In many of these cases the church is happy to provide them with God's will. Churches often have ministries that need extra hands, mission trips that need more volunteers, children's classes that need workers, and groups that need leaders. To facilitate this, they preach service, give ministry opportunities, and portray it as God's work.

Is it?

Is helping in our church's childcare what God wants from me? Perhaps it is, for God loves a servant. Or perhaps I've replaced God's leading with the leading of my church. Rather than spending the time to know the God I serve, I choose to serve the God I don't know. Yet, when did it happen that our church leaders determine our relationship with God. Perhaps it is more convenient to let someone else tell us what to do to be holy, than to take the time to figure it out for ourselves. Perhaps we feel like we can't figure it out, so we let someone else do that for us. If we're not careful, we'll find ourselves doing the "works of God" that He didn't want, because it was easier than taking the time to make Him Lord and find what He really desires.

Leads Us To Jesus

The Law was not written primarily to tell us how to live our life, but to lead us to the solution. It kept man from straying too far and paved the way for the real answer—Jesus.

> Therefore the Law has become our tutor to lead us to Christ, so that we may be justified by faith. — (Galatians 3:24)

Jesus put it this way.

> Do not think that I came to abolish the Law or the
> Prophets; I did not come to abolish but to fulfill. —
> (Matthew 5:17)

Jesus was the fulfillment of the law. The more you study the law, the more you'll find that it points to Jesus. His life and death fulfilled the law. It once for all paid the price that was needed. The law is not done away with now that Jesus has come. The law found its fulfillment in Him. How do I describe this? The law still stands, but in a new way. The methods that gave the ability for priests to come to God are changed into how we can come through Jesus. For example, blood had to be spilled for payment of sins. Animal sacrifice was only a temporary solution up until Jesus died and the last sin offering had been made. The law is still in effect but has been settled by Jesus. I suspect that each law is still in effect and has changed from the letter to the real spirit behind it.

Gospel

> For I am not ashamed of the gospel, for it is the power
> of God for salvation to everyone who believes. —
> (Romans 1:16)

Where the law had the power unto death, the gospel of grace has the power unto life. The reality of Jesus's gift is wonderful news, but do we treat it as we should? I remember going to my brother's house after one of his daughter's birthdays. Immediately after walking in, this sweet girl grabbed my wife by the hand and took us back to show us her birthday presents. She was so proud of her gifts that she couldn't help but share. That excitement even rubbed off on her younger sister who then ran back to retrieve another gift she had forgotten to show us. There was such a joy and excitement in their little faces about these amazing gifts. Honestly, can we say we act in this manner about Jesus? Is Jesus story "good news of great joy" for you? The Greek word that we translate as the gospel is *euaggelion*.

Typically, we translate this as "the good news", but if you really look, it translates close to something like "nearly too good to be true news."

> But if it is by grace, it is no longer on the basis of works, otherwise grace is no longer grace. — (Romans 11:6)

The whole purpose of grace is that it is a gift that we cannot earn. Grace is, by definition, "undeserved mercy or kindness". God gave us this gift. We have no way to earn it ourselves, that's why it was called the grace of God. As a gift, we may only receive this grace by accepting it for what it is.

> For by grace you have been saved through faith; and that not of yourselves, it is the gift of God; not as a result of works that no one may boast. — (Ephesians 2:8–9)

We must accept the fact that we are saved by grace alone. It's not by any works on our part. We are not saved by being selfless sometimes or by being kind to someone. We are not saved by following more laws than we break. We are helpless. It is all in His hands, and there is nothing we can do to fix this. He loved us enough to send His Son to die so that we can be reconciled to Him. If we can accept this, it changes everything. There is a freedom we find in grace to live.

Repentance And Faith

> If we confess our sins, He is faithful and righteous to forgive us our sins and to cleanse us from all unrighteousness. — (1 John 1:9)

Repentance is not only admitting that we have sinned, but confessing to God our desire to turn away from those sins and toward Him. Repentance is the only action we can take that is part of salvation. The rest is God. We put our faith in Him to save us. As the verse says, He is faithful to forgive if we are willing to confess.

The first foundation of our faith is that as we repent of our sins, God will provide grace.

> Now one of the Pharisees was requesting Him to dine with him, and He entered the Pharisee's house and reclined at the table. And there was a woman in the city who was a sinner; and when she learned that He was reclining at the table in the Pharisee's house, she brought an alabaster vial of perfume, and standing behind Him at His feet, weeping, she began to wet His feet with her tears, and kept wiping them with the hair of her head, and kissing His feet and anointing them with the perfume. Now when the Pharisee who had invited Him saw this, he said to himself, "If this man were a prophet He would know who and what sort of person this woman is who is touching Him, that she is a sinner." And Jesus answered him, "Simon, I have something to say to you." And he replied, "Say it, Teacher." "A moneylender had two debtors: one owed five hundred denarii, and the other fifty. "When they were unable to repay, he graciously forgave them both. So which of them will love him more?" Simon answered and said, "I suppose the one whom he forgave more." And He said to him, "You have judged correctly. — (Luke 7:36–43)

Afterward, Jesus spoke of the woman who had washed His feet saying:

> For this reason I say to you, her sins, which are many, have been forgiven, for she loved much; but he who is forgiven little, loves little. — (Luke 7:47)

This woman had a revelation concerning how much she had been forgiven. She was so convinced of the gift she received that she would honor Jesus in whatever way she could. Not only did she use a very costly perfume, but she also humbled herself among all the dinner guests—not caring what they thought—that she may honor the one who had forgiven her. The Pharisees could not understand her act. Their pride made it impossible for them to see this gift. Many of us don't understand either. It's taken me a long time to realize that this is the kind of love for God which I should possess. Knowing how important this act was, Jesus spoke these words of this woman.

> Truly I say to you, wherever this gospel is preached in the whole world, what this woman has done will also be spoken of in memory of her. — (Matthew 26:13)

Here we find real repentance. We can find this story included in all four of the Gospels. God wanted us to see a picture of what love should look like in return for His gift. He has forgiven so much that we can't do anything but love Him with all our heart for it. This is the love we miss. We spend so much time focused upon the world, that this grace doesn't spill over onto our everyday life. If we would just remember what all we have in the gospel, the access to God and His gifts, we will overflow with joy. Spreading the gospel becomes easy because it is so amazing.

> For I will forgive their iniquity, and their sin I will remember no more. — (Jeremiah 31:34)

When we repent of our sin, it is gone. God wipes it away. In this physical world we may still have the ramifications of our sins, but our spirit has been cleansed. Not only does God forgive us, He justifies us, so that it's as if the sin never happened. Religion tells us that sin holds God away from us; grace says that nothing can keep God away. Sin may keep God from being able to trust us with certain responsibilities and might keep us from coming to know Him better, but it can no longer keep us away from Him.

But he gives us more grace. — (James 4:6)

Much More Then

Consider the story of a friend of mine, we'll call him Larry.

Larry lived what should have been a good life. He had a wonderful wife and several sons. He was a successful executive at a large company, where he often would take trips overseas to handle operations. He had a big check, a big house, and a big life. Things were going well for Him, except for the small little fact that he wasn't happy. The signs were there if you knew where to look. On his trips he would often drink and party as the locations allowed. He became angry easily, had an uncontrolled tongue, and cared little for others' feelings. He knew he wasn't happy, but tried to live big enough to not think about it. Until that one day when a colleague badgered him into attending a Promise Keepers meeting. This is where He met Jesus and was saved.

After this, Larry knew what he had been missing. There was no doubt that he knew God was there now. He had gone to church in the past with his wife and kids, but now he went whenever he could. He knew the truth now and wanted to change his life. He heard someone talk about having a quiet time with the Lord every day, so he began to set aside time to read his Bible each day. It was hard, and he didn't seem to get much out of it, but he persisted. He heard another person say that he should journal, so he began to journal each day about his life and what he read in his Bible. It was tough, especially for a man's man to do. Even though he didn't notice any progress from this, again he persisted. In another case, he read of the fruits of the spirit in Galatians and realized he was not displaying many of them. Methodical as he was, he committed to begin showing more of the fruits of the spirit. It was hard going. One day he would try to be more patient, and of course would fail miserably. Another day he tried to be more loving, only to find himself snapping at colleagues at work. It didn't stop him though. He tried to rid himself of the bad habits of his past, each time with little success. He tried hard, but seemed to be making so little progress.

As with many of us, Larry had good intentions, but lived a frustrated life. I see these people all around me; men and women of good intentions that work hard to live a godly life, but can't break free from the world. We tend to look at these people and give them credit for trying, an "E for effort", we say. In fact, I've seen us celebrate their stories in church regarding how they are still failing but perservere.

The Lord has shown me that we are willing to receive grace to be saved, but after being saved, we tend to rely upon ourselves. I looked around and realized that we will ask God for help, but then we put on our WWJD bracelets, meet with our accountability partners, and celebrate recovery back from stumbling. We rely upon our own solutions and strength to overcome the enemy, rather than God's strength. The worst part is, we think we're relying upon God. We pray our prayers asking God to help us love Him more, to keep us from sinning, and to give us more strength; without realizing He already has. So, we fight and wonder why God isn't doing more to help us.

> But God demonstrates His own love toward us, in that while we were yet sinners, Christ died for us. — (Romans 5:8)

While still in sin, God paid the price. His love for us was this great. As great as this is, we cannot stop at this verse. We need to move on to the next two.

> Much more then, having now been justified by His blood, we shall be saved from the wrath of God through Him. For if while we were enemies we were reconciled to God through the death of His Son, much more, having been reconciled, we shall be saved by His life — (Romans 5:9–10)

We read these verses, but only see the results of Jesus's death, not His life. Jesus death was not the end of His gift. We were first reconciled to God through death, but then saved through his life. So often we stop at the death; believing that Jesus died for our sins and that we must suffer through this life to reach that promise. Fortunately, that's not all Jesus bought for us. Yes, God showed his love by dying for us, but after this God will continue to save us as we live our lives. The point we miss is that if in the depths of our sin God will save us, will He not do much more afterward to take care of His children?

> Therefore, as you have received Christ Jesus the Lord, so walk in him. — (Colossians 2:6)

How did we receive Christ? Through grace. So how shall we then walk in Him after our salvation? Again, through grace. As Christians, we have already accepted Jesus as our Lord and we feel like we can understand that grace; however, we have trouble accepting grace again as we live our lives. Just as our faith in the grace of God has saved us, that same faith in that same grace will lead us to a victorious life.

Grace Is For Action

> Therefore let us draw near with confidence to the throne of grace, so that we may receive mercy and find grace to help in time of need. — (Hebrews 4:16)

Grace is not only for forgiveness; grace is for action. The more I thought about it, the more I realized that grace is the provision for our need. It's the strength we need that we cannot provide ourselves. It's the help a father will provide to their child to help them succeed. It doesn't matter if the child deserves it or not, the father will help.

> Have we forgotten the mercy of a father
> Looking into a child's crying face,
> Or do we but see through scales
> As we sing of His amazing grace.

We help our children, often before they know to ask, and sometimes even without their agreement. When we're in need, we can know that God is the loving Father who provides for His children. Often, like a small child, we don't understand that the painful shot we're receiving is protecting us from a greater danger in the future. Even though the child doesn't want the shot, we're going to give it to them anyway. If we're willing to help when our children don't want it, how much more will we help when they ask for it? God will provide us the strength we need. When Paul was praying about his thorn, God responded that "His grace was sufficient". I suspect this is how Paul could make the following statement.

> For when I am weak, then I am strong.
> — (2 Corinthians 12:10)

As we rely upon the grace of God, His strength flows through us. This is how God wishes us to walk. He is not going to give us the strength and power in our bodies to overcome all our obstacles. Instead, He requires us to rely upon His strength in the time of trouble; to depend upon Him to provide for us. A part of grace is God's strength given to us to overcome this world.

> What then shall we say to these things? If God is for us, who is against us? He who did not spare His own Son, but delivered Him over for us all, how will he not also with Him freely give us all things? — (Romans 8:31-32)

If God was willing to give His Son for us, why do we think He would not also give us other things? God is good. Don't doubt that

God wants to help because things in your life became difficult. That's what this verse is saying; if God was willing to give His Son, will He not also give us many other things? This doesn't mean life will be easy from now on, but it should be much easier than we make it. God provides us with all we need, and freely gives us all things. We cannot earn grace. He gave us Jesus whom we did not deserve, and now He also gives us many other things; not because we deserve them, but because He loves us.

Law Of Liberty

> If you have died with Christ to the elementary principles of the world, why, as if you were living in the world, do you submit yourself to decrees, such as, 'Do not handle, do not taste, do not touch!' (which all refer to things destined to perish with use) – in accordance with the commandments and teachings of men. — (Colossians 2:20-22)

We're no longer under a law of no's; for that was the old law of sin and death. It was necessary for a time, but we have now come under a new covenant. We are under a grace that says "yes." I worry that we often forget this. We get caught under all the laws and expectations which we can never live up to. Through grace, God gives life to that which was dead.

> For sin shall not have dominion over you, for you are not under law but under grace. — (Romans 6:14)

Sin cannot control us anymore, as we are no longer under the old law.

> But one who looks intently at the perfect law, the law of liberty, and abides by it, not having become a

> forgetful hearer but an effectual doer, this man will be blessed in what he does. — (James 1:25)

Grace has become that perfect law. Greater than the Law of Moses, it not only brings direction, but freedom. If the glory of the law under Moses was so great that his face shown, what more does the perfect law of grace provide? Grace is the empowerment we need to do the works of God. Even from the beginning, we find there were two trees in the garden with Adam and Eve: the tree of life and the tree of the knowledge of good and evil. Eating from the second leads us to think we have done too much or too little, leading only to pride or condemnation. The tree of life is freedom. This is the tree full of grace and love for us. If we partake of it, we can be in the presence of the Lord rather than the dominion of the enemy.

No Condemnation

> There is now no condemnation for those who are in Christ Jesus — (Romans 8:1)

When I first read this (and actually thought about it), I assumed that I just misread the verse. How can I not feel condemned as the Bible tells me that my righteousness is like filthy rags? Strangely, this verse seems to be saying something different. Looking at the context, we find it between two well-known chapters of Romans. In Romans 7, Paul speaks of living life in our own strength, and how we will fail much like Larry's story above. In Romans 8, Paul speaks about a successful life living through the spirit. Right in the middle is this verse. What I've come to realize is that I have been missing out. I spent too much of my time in shame, regret, and condemnation for my actions. I assumed that if I didn't feel condemned, I must not be listening to God, because I am a horrible sinner. Fortunately, the Word of God disagrees.

Consider what happens when you hurt a friend or spouse. How do you act when you come before them and they know what you have done? You look down. You talk quietly. You basically try to hide. My wife likes to say I'm "pouting" in situations like this. I would like to make it clear that as a grown man I do not pout. Grown men internalize… quietly… with a grumpy face. Back to the point, my shame at what I've done leads me to avoid talking. If the person I hurt tries to love me, I feel like I don't even deserve it, so I don't accept it. Basically, the relationship is put on hold until I can get over myself and my shame.

> For everyone who does evil hates the Light, and does not come to the Light for fear that his deeds will be exposed. — (John 3:20)

As such, we create relationships of regret and shame. In my own marriage, I find myself trying to attain to some goal, to perform well enough for what I believe I should be doing. That's because my focus strays from a relationship of love to one of performance. Don't misunderstand me here; I have a wonderful loving wife who still loves me despite all my shortcomings. What I've done is put a burden upon myself that she did not. I haven't failed her, but instead I have failed the role I created for myself. Think back to what I said about the Law. Why do we try so hard to look like a good Christian? Are we avoiding sin because it's wrong or because we believe we will be punished? Do we fear grieving our Father or letting down those around us? Since we keep sinning, we wonder how God could love us right now. Maybe later, after we've proved ourselves, He could love us again. What we don't realize is God still wants relationship with us even during these times. The bottom line is that when we sit in shame and condemnation, we cannot hear His voice.

Paul wanted to let us know that God is no longer condemning us. This means that when you're listening to condemnation, you're not listening to God. That leaves one of two choices. Either you're listening to yourself or to the devil. In a strange way, our sins make grace all the more amazing. We don't live in condemnation of sin, just remembrance. Jesus took us past that. If we're focused on our sin, it makes doing the right thing that much harder.

Something I've learned from experience is that God would rather be in the loop through our mistakes, than to have us push Him away because of them. He's forgiven us so much, He's not going to shut us down just because we fell one more time. It is impossible to continue to walk with the Lord if we aren't listening to Him because of shame. We must seek relationship His way, not ours. We should walk forward with our lives remembering His love, for perfect love drives out fear. Condemnation will tell you "you can't, you won't, you aren't worth it"; but God's grace is saying, "I took care of it before you even asked." Don't let shame pull you down when grace was already given. There's a song by Shane and Shane that I love; it's called "Embracing Accusation." The chorus says that the devil is preaching to us that we are cursed and have gone astray. The devil is happy to show up and tell you that you have gone astray and can't make your way back. He'll remind you of your sins, your shortcomings, and ask how God could ever use someone like you. What we need to realize is in the final verse of the song. The devil keeps signing the same "song" to us over and over, but forgets the last part of the song: Jesus saves.

Think of this the next time you are reminded of something wrong you did and feel condemned. The devil is trying to condemn you because of how you failed, but while doing this, he is inadvertently reminding you that Jesus is ever more wonderful for taking care of it. So instead of focusing on how helpless you are, focus on how good God is. Take that failure to God and tell Him, "Lord, I'm so sorry I did this again, and I want to improve, but thank you so much for Your grace, which has forgiven and accepted me even now. You are wonderful!" Capture each thought of shame, and rather than allowing them to pull you down, use that same failure to rejoice that God's grace is so much bigger than your sins.

Grace Abounds

> The Law came in so that the transgression would increase, but where s3in increased, grace abounded all the more. — (Romans 5:20)

As time goes on you will use this grace to find freedom from those sins. Strangely, I often feel the Lord's presence the most when I repent. I believe that humility of spirit we have in repentance draws God near. I imagine the fragrance of repentance is a perfume He cannot resist. Remember that if you've repented from your sins, God has removed them. Freedom is wonderful. It's a longing built into each of us. Do not waste time on something that God has moved past. Listen to Paul's words from Philippians.

> Brethren, I do not regard myself as having laid hold of it yet; but one thing I do: forgetting what lies behind and reaching forward to what lies ahead, I press on toward the goal for the prize of the upward call of God in Christ Jesus. — (Philippians 3:13-14)

Let's stop living in the failures of our past, or in second guessing our decisions, and move forward to what lies ahead of us; to the hope of His calling. Forget regret, it holds no power for us and it will provide no help. Think back to what Jesus did. He was called a "friend of sinners" in Matthew 11:9, for Jesus would rather have spent time with the broken that know they need help, than with the self-righteous that were too blind to ask.

This is the type of grace I try to live under.

> For the grace of God that brings salvation has appeared to all men. It teaches us to say "No" to ungodliness and worldly passions, and to live self-controlled, upright and godly lives in this present age, while we wait for

> the blessed hope-the glorious appearing of our great God and Savior, Jesus Christ. — (Titus 2:11–13)

True grace doesn't set us free to sin more, but sets us free to live holier. True grace teaches us to say no to the world and yes to God.

Oh yeah, and let's not forget about Larry. Larry finally found the revelation that it was not in his attempts at being godly, but abiding with God that made all the difference. He found this in a men's disciple group he was invited to. As he began to live that relationship focused life of grace, he led many more of these groups himself and touched many other men's lives with his passion for God. Since then other ministry opportunities have opened for him to reach to the lost and broken who need God's grace.

Faith is a Substance

Live By Faith

For we walk by faith, not by sight. — (2 Corinthians 5:7)

At many points in my life I have found myself asking God the same question. "Father, rather than me waiting, trying to trust in you and trying to walk without knowing my direction, why don't You just tell me what to do in [insert life changing decision here]?" One time this was choosing a college, another time was whom to marry, then buying a house, and next choosing jobs. In each case I've found myself in a similar situation. I asked God what I should do—trying to follow His direction—but I wasn't sure which way to go. I was trying to trust in God and have confidence that He would guide me, but I kept feeling like I was coming up a little short. Not that I would give up, but I began to worry. I wanted to be told what to do. Most likely you have felt the same. Why wouldn't God just write the answer in the sky for us to read so we knew what to do. This approach would make life much simpler and easier to have such a clear answer. At least, that is what I believed until the day the Lord answered me.

"But if I told you, how would you grow in faith?"

Oh.

Why then does God make it like this; where we need to come to Him through faith? Personally, I think it's love. I believe this for several reasons, but first let's imagine if God acted like I wanted. Each time we ask, God's voice booms across the sky; fire and lightning coming from the clouds like at Mount Sinai. There's no denying that God has answered my request. There's also no choice either. God could clearly make happen what He desires, so who would dare disobey? Would that engender love or fear? I believe most of us would obey out of fear, which would inevitably lead to resentment from being told what to do with no choice.

Maturity requires faith. When God does something, always keep in mind that God is love. This tells us that faith must be a better way. God has our best interests in mind. We learn to trust Him in the small ways and follow His leading as He carefully directs us upon the path. Not only this, but we need faith over experience. Many of us learn the most through experience. That's the nice way of saying we don't get it right at first and learn the hard way. Learning from experience is one reason we have such trouble believing that God loves us as much as He does. We look back at our lives and remember all the bad experiences; wondering where God was in those. If He let that happen to us, then maybe He's not what we think. Experience tells us life is hard and we should just deal with it. Faith tells us that God has a plan and is using this to help us.

Good Pleasure

> For it is God who is at work in you, both to will and to work for His good pleasure. — (Philippians 2:13)

Make sure you get this. God is the one working in you, not you. You cannot do this. No amount of effort on your part will make your life better, will save the lost, or will bring you to God. It just can't be done. It's God working in you through faith. You do join in the work, but honestly, you don't have much to contribute. I know I still don't fully get this, because I find myself struggling so much to be good. Rather than just realizing that it is "Christ in me," I try being like Christ. Rather, He does it in us for His good pleasure. Do you know what gives the Father good pleasure?

> Fear not, little flock; for it is your Father's good pleasure to give you the kingdom. — (Luke 12:32)

The kingdom, the place where God reigns. Not only does He

reign, but He pours out His gifts and He works on behalf of His people. This is a land of miracles, of angels and saints, and of God's works. He wants to give that to you. It's not in payment for your actions nor in agreement with some deal, but merely because He enjoys it. He loves to pour out His gifts on His people. How do we receive these gifts? You got it, through faith.

Without Faith It Is Impossible To Please God

> And without faith it is impossible to please Him, for he who comes to God must believe that He is and that He is a rewarder of those who seek him. — (Hebrews 11:6)

How can we come into the presence of our God—who is a spirit—if we look only at the natural? How can we learn to walk with the Lord unless we first move in what we cannot see? We must begin to make our choices with what faith tells us and not what our eyes show us. This means we will do things that don't seem to make sense. Perhaps it's staying home a certain night to spend in prayer rather than going to watch the game. It could be sacrificing you free time after the kids go to sleep so you can get up early to have time with God. It could even be as simple as reading the Bible rather than a book. What do you really believe? If God were that real and important to us, then we would search Him out until we found Him. If my faith ruled me, I would spend more of my life on my knees and less on my couch.

Even as I'm writing this chapter, for the first time I really caught that last part of Hebrews 11:6. Did that actually just define faith for me personally? "Believe that God is, and that He rewards those who seek Him." Notice that it didn't say faith is witnessing to the lost. It also didn't say faith is wearing a WWJD bracelet (oops, I just dated myself). Even more it didn't say faith was participating in church activities. In fact, this is the opposite of how I would normally see faith defined. According to this scripture, faith is believing that God exists and looking for Him. It's internal. Faith is about what you do on the inside, not what you do outside. Our faith will then result in works and in changed lives, but it's about the internal choices and the relationship more than the works themselves.

Will He Find Faith

> However, when the Son of Man comes, will he find faith on the earth? — (Luke 18:8b)

When the Lord looks at you, what does He see? Will He find you faithful toward Him, following the rules, or just unfaithful? Does your life show faith in the person, or that you merely follow directions? There is a difference here. A servant follows directions, but God wants more than for us to be servants. Like I said, fear can lead your decisions as well. Does your life change those around you and act as a living testimony of the goodness of God? Put simply, is God proud of how you are living now?

Righteous Live By Faith

Consider Abraham. He believed in the promise God gave him for 80 years before it came to pass. He and Sarah were way past the age at which they should be able to have children, yet God's word was true.

> Then he believed in the LORD; and He reckoned it to him as righteousness. — (Genesis 15:6)

Abraham's faith made him righteous. It wasn't following the law that made him righteous, nor was it being perfect. No, Abraham believed in God and that was it. By believing in God and holding firm, he found himself in right standing with God. This is how we must live. It is not through our understanding and wisdom, or through convincing ourselves of how real God is that makes us walk with God; it is through faith in a God who loves us.

> But the righteous will live by his faith. — (Habakkuk 2:4b)

Faith is the path of righteousness. As we walk in faith, we begin to understand the God we believe in. God did not lay out a path before us with a map and instruction manual. Had He done that, then it wouldn't require faith which is vital to our growth. If we had that physical proof we desire, then it would come down to logic and not trust.

What Is Faith

> And of faith in God — (Hebrews 6:1b)

Paul's second foundation he gave in Hebrews was faith. Now that we've run all around this topic, let's get back to the basics of faith itself. Romans tells us that the righteous *"live by faith"*. Those three words tell us more than we might initially think. Of course we live by faith, as we know that Jesus died and we didn't see that; so it is by faith that we believe. We tend to consider our faith as believing that Jesus died to save us. The difference here is that it didn't say that we are saved by faith, but that we live by it.

> So then, just as you received Christ Jesus as Lord, continue to live your lives in him. — (Colossians 2:17)

This rules out believing in what we see. Faith in Christ for salvation means believing the word of God over what we understand and see. This means the same faith we used for salvation, is the same faith we use to walk forward in life. We make choices in our life based upon faith in the Word.

More Than Belief

> And He said to them, "Because of the littleness of your faith; for truly I say to you, if you have faith the size of a mustard seed, you will say to this mountain, 'Move from here to there,' and it will move; and nothing will be impossible to you. — (Matthew 17:20)

Faith is more than just belief. Let me give an example of this. I remember once when I was about 11 years old, I had heard the scripture above and decided to try this out. We had an old computer that had stopped working. I think it had finally overheated and something had fried inside. At that age, this computer was very important to me. I remember sitting on my bed, looking at this computer and believing it to work again. I believe if I "had faith" like this verse said, then God would fix the computer. So, I would convince my mind it's going to work, then I'd go click the button. Guess what? It didn't. Seems silly, but at the same time we often do similar things to scriptures. We take a part of them and try to make that true without understanding them. What I didn't understand at the time is that faith isn't just belief in something; it's belief in the word of God. Whether this be the written word or the spoken word, it's our faith in the words that come from God that let God move. I realized after I gave it some thought that if it was just belief, then those with mental disorders who are convinced they live in a different world would get better results than any of us.

> But someone will say, "You have faith; I have deeds."
> Show me your faith without deeds, and I will show
> you my faith by my deeds. — (James 2:18)

Faith is not convincing ourselves of God. Faith is not a belief, but something more. We believe in God, that's good, but there's more to it. When we need to do something that can only be accomplished if God does it, that's where faith comes in. Belief tells us there is a god, trust tells us He loves us and will take care of us, but faith makes us walk on water.

Faith Is A Substance

> Now faith is the substance of things hoped for, the evidence of things not seen. — (Hebrews 11:1)

Faith is the *substance* of things hoped for. Why do I like this? Because it helps to get across a part of faith that we often forget. Like I've said, faith isn't just belief, faith isn't just a choice, faith isn't just hope for something—faith is the substance of the thing. Faith is the reality of the truth we know. There's that witty little poster I've seen before of a kid with an umbrella, and the saying at the bottom goes something like "Hope is praying for rain, faith is buying an umbrella." That's close, but not it. Faith is more like us opening the umbrella, which then causes the rain to come. Had you not bought the umbrella and opened it, the rain wouldn't come. Why? I have no idea. Ask the Lord. We don't have faith in something we hope will happen, faith tells us it is already done, and so we have the confidence to go ahead.

Again, faith is not a choice. It's not based on reason, as that is logic. Faith is the substance of hope. We have hope in our hearts because of Jesus. Faith takes that hope and makes it real. Faith is what lets you know that spending the time with your Father is better than with your TV. Faith leads you to pick out that stranger and tell them something the Lord has placed on your heart for them. Faith is what speaks to you in the night convincing you that the kingdom is here and working around you.

Our faith lets us know of the Father and the kingdom. Our faith lets us feel and see that they exist, giving us evidence of the truth of it all. It comforts us in our doubts and encourages us in our actions. This is how those persecuted can rejoice, because they can know of those things unseen, and rejoice at what is coming.

Finding Faith

Where then do we find faith? If faith does all of this, how do we come across it? It's simple.

> So faith comes from hearing, and hearing by the word of Christ. — (Romans 10:17)

There is truth in the Word. The Word is made real to us by revelation. Revelation comes as it's spoken into our lives. When I say spoken, there are several paths that can take. God can speak to us through the Bible, through others, or even directly into our hearts. Yet, we can only receive if we are listening. It really is this simple. If we're listening and attentive, we can hear the truth. The truth is revealed and stirs up faith. We take that faith and as we apply it to our lives, the physical world moves to accommodate the kingdom of God.

Faith Is Power

> For the kingdom of God does not consist in words but in power. — (1 Corinthians 3:20)

Tell me, where is the power of the kingdom around us? Do you see it? For too much of my life I've taken for granted the power of God and worked under my own power. Our churches often plan around what we believe to be God's ability. It disheartens me when I hear some people speak concerning what they consider are miracles these days. In one such instance, the miracle was a gift given to the church so it could expand. Does that mean a big gift in a timely manner is a miracle? I guess if you get down to it, it probably is, but it was also just a person with money providing for the church. When I look in Acts and see the miracles that occur there, I see something different. These are miracles that man could not do. I think of the blind seeing, the sick being healed, of the physical world bowing to the spiritual. This is the kingdom of God coming upon the earth.

Faith is the appropriation of God's will in the spiritual realm that we bring to the physical.

Victory To Overcome The World

> And this is the victory that has overcome the world – our faith. — (1 John 4:5b)

I love reading the scriptures that speak of overcoming, because it brings me hope. I see all the things I've struggled with over the years, and realize I don't have to keep struggling. Do you believe that we can overcome? Often we don't want to upset people so we preach how we have to struggle and struggle with sin, but that's not what I read in the Word. I see the Bible telling me that I can overcome the enemy. I read that we are "more than conquerors" (Romans 8:37). God has shown us the way to overcome—our faith. We have only to take it, and to make it more important than those other things. There is no question that God has commanded us to not sin. Have faith that His word is true and stop sinning. If we do this, the ability to reach higher is right there. It's so simple.

Writing This Book

Writing this book is one of my tests of faith. I have spent so much time writing something that may never go past my computer screen. It's not like I'm an author. You see, no one even knows me. I'm a computer programmer by career. Just another in a sea of faces. Every time I sit down to write, it's faith that drives me on. I must make a choice on whether I believe or not, yet even that's not fully faith. I have hope that what I'm writing will make a difference, but hope doesn't move me. It's the faith that God has called me to write, called me to put into words the truths He's taught me. That faith doesn't always make sense, but it keeps moving. This is the same sort of faith that Peter showed when all the crowds left Jesus side. Jesus had just finished talking about how they must eat His flesh and drink His blood. Not exactly a call for the weak of heart. As the crowds began to leave, we find this interaction.

> So Jesus said to the twelve, "You do not want to go away also, do you?" Simon Peter answered Him, "Lord, to whom shall we go? You have words of eternal life. — (John 6:67–68)

Faith isn't necessarily pretty, but it drives you. I'm fairly confident Peter was confused and didn't understand what was going on. He probably didn't even like what he was hearing, but the truth drove him. Sometimes with this book I get stuck or stop writing for a time. Sometimes I look at myself and think, "who am I to write anything?" Yet faith drives me on. If God could call me, I must respond. God once said to me, "Unless you use your faith, I cannot give you more." Use what you have, and leave it to the Lord to figure out the rest.

Use It Or Lose It

Let me give you a little warning from my own experience here. When God gives you revelation, He also gives you the faith to use it. I've seen this on several occasions. God shows me something in His word I could live toward, and in my excitement I grab hold, only to drop away after it gets rough. Unfortunately, what I've found is that it's harder to take hold of it later. I believe that with the initial "deposit" of faith from the Lord, there is much grace for you to take and move forward with that truth. Afterward, it seems like you must work harder to see the results.

Be Holy

> Therefore He says: God resists the proud, but gives grace to the humble. — (James 4:6)

Here we find one of those key verses in our relationship with God. The part of the verse that touches me is not what we might do, but how God reacts to us. We know that we should be humble and not proud, but did you ever think about what it means for God to resist the proud. Wow. Can you imagine? We're not talking about a coworker causing you a problem or a family member stirring up trouble; this is the God who created the universe resisting you. How do you think that will go for you? Who do you think is going to win? Seriously, it's a bit terrifying to think of God resisting me. The truth I take from this verse is that if I want anything to do with God, pride can have no place in me. Pride is the first of the seven sins mentioned in Proverbs 6 that are detestable to the Lord. The antidote for pride is humility, which we find back at the beginning of Jesus's teaching.

> Blessed are the poor in spirit, for theirs is the kingdom of heaven. — (Matthew 5:3)

The first beatitude Jesus spoke during the Sermon on the Mount was about humility. As we dig further, we find that humility is one of the pre-requisites to have anything to do with the kingdom.

> Truly I tell you, unless you change and become like little children, you will never enter the kingdom of heaven. — (Matthew 18:3)

The humility I speak of is not the showy humility of the Pharisees, who proclaim their love and sacrifices to God for all in order to be noticed by others. Neither is it the humility of the insecure, who are terrified to do anything when someone is watching. This false humility is in fact an excess of pride; pride from trying so hard to not look bad before others. No, I speak of the humility you find in those who understand who they are. The humility you find in yourself after you've fallen. The same humility that I found after I spent a day in self-pity for a specific sin I fell into. The humility I found as I finally brought myself low to come before the Lord the next day, knowing I've messed up. I didn't make excuses, I just sat there in my filth and said, "I'm sorry". To my surprise, I immediately felt myself in His presence and I couldn't imagine why. Why after what I've done and how long I spent wallowing would I feel His love? So I asked, and His answer to me was simple: "I draw near to the humble."

It was at this point that I realized something new. I often shy away from coming to God when I sin. The problem this raises is that I can rarely come before him in purity, because I mess up too often. Yet, that is what Jesus's blood does for us; it covers our sin. What I should bring to God is the humility to know that I am a sinner and I am saved by grace. This is what allows me into His presence. This is not a freedom to sin, but a drive to cleanse myself from sin. If I'm to be humble and honest, then I must be repentant of my sin and so be covered by grace to come before Him. The actions that separate me from God are not the small acts of impetuous sins, but the repetitive sins which I don't want to repent of—the ones I keep repeating and don't move past. As long as we live in repentance, we are righteous and can come before the Lord. We are who we are only because the Lord has chosen us; because He has mercy on us.

This is not the only path to humility. We tend to only look at humility as our response for all the bad things we have done, but that's just a part. Humility is in fact not about sin. That may seem like an odd statement, but it's true. I say this, for Jesus was humble. Look at this passage from the last supper.

> Jesus, knowing that the Father had given all things into His hands, and that He had come forth from God and was going back to God, got up from supper,

> and laid aside His garments; and taking a towel, He girded Himself. — (John 13:3–4)

How was it that Jesus could take aside everything and humble himself this way? The Prince of Peace was to come on His knees and wipe the dirty feet of men who would soon leave Him in His hour of trial. This verse tells us that His humility was rooted in knowing where He came from and where He was going. The same is true for us. This knowledge shows us our place. We came from God and we are going back to God. We are His. This truth frees us to not worry about ourselves. When I come in humility to God, I leave changed. I don't know how many times I have come before the Lord and opened my heart, only to find that I'm holding a grudge against someone and must let it go. Unforgiveness will block our path, as will pride and selfishness. When we come to the Lord in openness, the Spirit will reveal to us things that are hindering us. Then we must be willing to be nothing before Him, to follow, to listen, and to obey. His way is better than ours.

Let's talk about an example that is easier to relate to. Looking back upon my experiences at work, I find that I can work with people who need help. I spent around 15 years at one company, moving my way into a senior position where I worked with plenty of new employees. Some of them came with humility. They may have thought they knew how to do things, but they were open to the prospect of being wrong. Those would recognize the experience and knowledge I had and were willing to listen; even when I occasionally sent them off on the wrong course. Then there are the others. These came into a position knowing exactly what's wrong and how they would fix it. I found that many of these would wander off trying to fix things that didn't need to be done. They tended to know a better way to do something and were quick to criticize others' work. They would focus more on the problems than on solutions. It's much easier to say someone has a problem than to show you can solve it. Working with this group was difficult. Often, I hadn't even finished describing the work I would want done before they would jump in to tell me how it should be done. If they had some clue what they're doing, they would figure it out and at least get some work done. Most of the time, they would just end up in a position where they found themselves unable to finish and with a lead developer too irritated with them to take the time to help them get it right. Understand, I am more patient than most of my colleagues, as I could handle working with most people including tough customers, but a person with this sort of silly pride was the only type of person I would tend to completely give up on and let them fail.

Looking back, I realize this was similar to Jesus's view of the Pharisees. They knew better than Him, and they knew better than everyone else. When you think you know that much, you can't be open to hear anything. Often, Jesus didn't even waste His time on them. Perhaps I can understand why God resists the proud, because I find that I do the same thing.

Openness

Openness is another key to our relationship with the Lord. When we come before Him in prayer and in worship, we must lay our hearts bare before Him. We should open up completely to Him—for we are who we are—and there is no sense in hiding or holding back from the One who knows it all. My path down this revelation began with a minister speaking on the subject of openness, which I admit took me a while to understand. The Holy Spirit continued to nudge me that this was very important, so I spent some time dwelling on it. Over the next few days it began to sink in more and more.

During this period when I would come to the Lord in prayer, I made a point to first stop and try to open up my heart. Think of it as trying reveal all of my soul before the Lord. There's no pretense or memorized prayers. I would quietly come before the Lord telling Him that this is who I am and showing Him my faults, which we both know are there. I might pray something like, "I want more of you, but I keep doing this." "Thank you for your mercy as always even when I don't do what I wish." Know what I found? When there's openness and honesty, it leads to holiness. When I'm honest with myself and with God, I can't continue in my sin. As long as I continue pretending to myself that I am not in sin or trying to ignore it, I'll stay there. However, being honest before the Lord is to also be honest with myself. When I come like this, I repent. I mean seriously, how can you come before the living God saying, "here is my sin, but I think I'll keep doing it." Instead I found myself in a new walk. Ever since this point, I have trouble coming before God without openness. If I know there's something between us, I can't pretend anymore. For years I had done the old way, saying my prayers while pretending my heart was in it. I would act like certain areas of my life weren't there as I read off my prayer lists to God. Now if there is a sin which I am holding onto, I can't pretend in my prayers anymore. I found that God wants more from me when I came to that point that I realized I was acting out a relationship instead of having one. When you hit that, you have no choice but to be open; for there's no other option.

A Relationship Of Holiness

Holiness was never a common topic in the churches where I have been a member. I was taught about doing the right things, following the commandments, and being good, but I was not taught about holiness. Holiness was a God thing. I've always known that we should do the right thing, because that's what God wants us to do. I think I knew in some way that the better I was, the more pleased He would be; yet I've been taught grace so heavily that it's hard to know the line between righteousness and holiness. It's more like we're shooting for a cutoff. Somewhere good enough that we can be confident in our salvation by the fruit expressed in our lives, but not so good that we have to give up too much or try too hard. Far be it that we inconvenience ourselves for God.

Then I began considering holiness more deeply. Want to know the simplest way to go searching for a topic? The internet. I pulled up a Bible website, typed in holiness, and away I went. As I started walking through the verses that mentioned the word "holiness", I ran across this one that caught my eye.

> Therefore, having these promises, beloved, let us cleanse ourselves from all defilement of flesh and spirit, perfecting holiness in the fear of God.— (2 Corinthians 7:1)

That's interesting. Since we have "these promises", we should be holy. This was the type of thing I was looking for. Here we are told there is a reason for us to pursue holiness in our lives. Let's step back a couple verses and find out what that reason is.

> Or what agreement has the temple of God with idols? For we are the temple of the living God; just as God said, "I will dwell in them and walk among them; And I will be their God, and they shall be My people. Therefore, come out from their midst and be separate," says the Lord. "And do not touch what is unclean; and I will welcome you. And I will be a father to you, and you shall be sons and daughters to Me," says the Lord Almighty.— (2 Corinthians 6:16–18)

At this point, I feel the need to be honest. When I read that, it just went over my head. I remember thinking, what in the world do these statements have in relation to holiness. I'm not exactly sure why it didn't sink in. In fact, I nearly moved on, but decided to add it to my list. I keep a list of passages to meditate on. Things that I found interesting and want to go back over. Many of them have ended up in this book. So, to practice what I preach, I memorized it and then spent some time meditating upon it.

First truth, I love the idea of God saying that we will be part of His people. As a part of His people, He will dwell in us and walk alongside us. What a promise! Then it gets even better. Not only that, but He goes on to say He will be a father to us, and we will be sons and daughters to Him. Think about this for a minute. He will be our father. Tell me, what child doesn't know his father well? Typically, the child will live with his father, hear his voice often, and see him consistently. Do we live with God like that? We seem to live with a birth certificate that tells us the name of the father, but we don't live with Him each day. This sounds more like an orphan than a child, but Jesus told us He would not leave us as orphans. Even more, the verse continues to say that we are not only children, but "sons". This isn't the word for a child, but the word used for a son ready for his inheritance. Let's be honest with ourselves here. It's about time we actually believe the Bible. If the word says we will be God's people and He will dwell in us, walk with us, and be our Father; don't you think we would actually know Him? We're back to my recurring issue here with much of Christianity right now. We don't know God. We "spiritually" know Him, as in, we have faith in the Word, but many of us don't live past that. We don't talk with Him, see Him, or move in His presence. Instead, we guess, we hope, and we blindly wander about trying to do His will. If we can be honest, the life we live is not what He promised.

What then was the promise in 2 Corinthian 6? That if we come out from the midst of the world and don't touch what is unclean, then we will be His children. God wants to create a relationship with us. Coming back to the original verse, let's look again how Paul finished off this passage. "Therefore, having these promises, beloved, let us cleanse ourselves from all defilement of flesh and spirit, perfecting holiness in the fear of God." The natural result of having these promises is to cleanse ourselves and be holy. Let me simplify this all down into one simple statement.

The basis of our relationship with God is holiness.

If we want to hear his voice, we better practice holiness. If we want to walk in His courts, holiness. If we want to see God("blessed are the pure in heart for they shall see God"), holiness.

Be holy, for I am holy. — (1 Peter 1:16)

We have a habit of putting holiness on a pedestal that can never be reached. Yet, if it couldn't be done, why would Paul tell us to perfect holiness rather than telling us to try to be holy. Holiness is not only possible, it is necessary. As I was spending time learning from the Lord on this, there was a little equation that popped into my head as I was praying. These three attributes being the basis for practicing holiness. I have no scriptural basis for this part, so take it with a grain of salt.

Holiness = HOnesty + humiLIty + brokeNESS

I'm more convinced than ever that holiness is a deal breaker. We have dirtied our Christianity to make it ok to struggle with sins; justifying why we can never get past our old man. What we have forgotten is that as we disregard the sacrifice of Christ, we dirty His blood. He paid a price for us to be free and we count it less significant than our petty indulgences. Our salvation is not that of lordship, but of convenience and safety. God called us to be holy so we could be like Him. Our relationship is based on what we have in common, and that is holiness. As we set ourselves apart from the world, we become more like Christ. As we become like Him, He in turn draws near to us. In contrast, as we continue in sin, we cannot grow and we cannot hear. We sentence ourselves to the same place we have always been.

God is available for a personal relationship. Not a "Sunday school answer" relationship, but a real and intimate one. A relationship where we can talk to each other, see each other, and get to know each other. God desires this, but we don't. We've become so convinced that our pageantry is relationship, that we cannot climb out of the hole we dug for ourselves. We think we are rich, but we are poor. We think we know so much, yet we haven't realized that we don't even know Him. He is the bread of life. He is the giver and the sustainer of life itself, but we've convinced ourselves that life is enjoying what we have rather than knowing the one who made it. Don't you think life should involve Him who created it, not just the drama we have created around Him.

> Stop bringing meaningless offerings! Your incense is detestable to me. New Moons, Sabbaths and convocations-- I cannot bear your worthless assemblies. Your New Moon feasts and your appointed festivals I hate with all my being. They have become a burden to me; I am weary of bearing them. — (Isaiah 1:13–14)

Beware building your relationship upon traditions and interpretations rather than upon relationship. You can see God's thoughts on a life lived that way. Our relationship with God is bounded upon holiness. Be willing to set aside all your sins, all the things that pull you from God, and go see for yourself how you will grow. Take a chance, do that which you know to do and continue in it.

Sanctification

How then do we become holy? We get there through the process of sanctification. Again, I have heard few messages on sanctification. I had to go looking for myself to find much on this topic. First, I ran across John Wesley, who is known as the founder of the Methodists and one of the Reformers. I read his book "A Plain account of Christian Perfection." There I found the belief that a Christian could actually reach a point of perfection in this life where they are free from sin. I know one of the main arguments against is that that we cannot be perfect. No one can but God. The problem I find with that which I've yet to hear a good response is that God wouldn't tell us to "be perfect" if it was impossible. Still, I wasn't ready for this at the time. Since then, I've come to realize how sanctification—the pursuit of holiness—is key in building that relationship with God. It's not that you are becoming sinless, but that you are becoming free from sin. Jesus said that sin had no hold on Him. The idea is to reach that point where we are not pulled away by sin. We may still sin at points, but we quickly confess and get things right because we are not so easily entangled anymore.

> So that He might sanctify her, having cleansed her by the washing of water with the word. — (Ephesians 5:25)

The context for this verse pertains to a husband loving and helping his wife, but it gives us the truth we need still. Besides, we're to be the bride of Christ. Sanctification is the washing away of our filth: sins, the old man, and the world. The washings of the Old Testament were in preparation to come before God, which matches up with sanctification. We are washed by the word of God. The truths we've learned lead us upon the path. The word of God made alive in our hearts gives us the power to be free. Want to be free? Then fill yourself with the Word of God. Study it, meditate, memorize, and hope in it.

> Now when Abram was ninety-nine years old, the LORD appeared to Abram and said to him, "I am God Almighty; Walk before Me, and be blameless. I will establish My covenant between Me and you, And I will multiply you exceedingly." — (Genesis 17:1–2)

God comes to Abraham and asks two things: walk before Him and be blameless. Again, a core part of the covenant between God and Abraham was holiness. We must become like the Lord.

> For this is the will of God, your sanctification. — (1 Thessalonians 4:3)

First, though, we must go to war with sin. There's no time left for us to dilly-dally around like we have in the past. If we are not willing to clean ourselves up, we will not move ahead. I am ready to move ahead. This isn't a small decision or a little pact you make. This is war.

The first and most obvious step is the habitual sins in our life, things we will come back to over and over again. These are the sins with no excuse. We have fallen here before, we know it is wrong, and we come back. That must go first. The obvious ones here are addictions, idolatries, selfishness, etc. Yet we must go even past this. We must clean up the glaring issues so that our heart may change and we can work on our reactions. Things like our temper, anger, feelings of hurt, pride. These are those that lie beneath the surface, then jump up and strike before we realize what happened. They must go as well. If you have a tendency to sin in a certain area, put it far away. Do not think on it and do not entertain it. Sin is the enemy. There is no room for greyness, but rather a call to take a stand and live for God. We're told that our bodies are the temple of God, but they are too dirty for Him to take up residence. We want to be clean enough that God can dwell in us; that He can entrust us to move forward. After removing sin we then move on to obedience and the bond-servant relationship.

As you progress past this, God will begin to prune you as a vinedresser prunes a plant. You can find this described in John 15. God will prune away the excesses and the unnecessary parts. All the little things in our lives that even though they aren't sin, they also aren't of God. To go deeper is to give up more. As He prunes, you become more and more like Him.

> But now having been freed from sin and enslaved to God, you derive your benefit, resulting in sanctification, and the outcome, eternal life. — (Romans 6:22)

We have already spoken of eternal life. This isn't just salvation. Salvation does not require holiness. No, eternal life is knowing God. That means according to Paul, sanctification leads you to that level of relationship with the Lord. This is the singular vision of my whole book and my life. Knowing Him. It is a quest to find Him. The Bible assures us that He can be found.

The Spirit

The Helper

> I will ask the Father, and He will give you another Helper, that He may be with you forever. — (John 14:16)

On the night before His arrest, Jesus eats the Last Supper with His disciples, washes their feet, and then takes them out to the garden of Gethsemane. These actions were taken to prepare His disciples for what was to come. He would soon be arrested and His disciples scattered, so now was His last chance to impart to them that which was necessary. It was during this period that Jesus taught them concerning the coming of the Holy Spirit and what the Holy Spirit would do for them. Jesus wanted to make this clear before He left. Keep in mind, they've been following Him for three years. How were they going to handle being alone? They weren't ready to be let loose on their own if they were to change the world. They needed help.

Better To Have The Spirit

> But I tell you the truth, it is to your advantage that I go away; for if I do not go away, the Helper will not come to you; but if I go, I will send Him to you. — (John 16:7)

I must admit, for a long time I read this verse and mentally shrugged. I imagined walking with Jesus as the disciples did; seeing Him heal the sick, walk on water, and feed the crowds. I can remember some of my prayers, where I would tell God that if I could have just seen a few of these acts I would have more faith. Have you not thought the same? Now the Bible tells me that having the Spirit here—which I have had available for over twenty years—would be better than walking with Jesus while He was on the earth? If I'm to judge based on my experience, then my answer would be no. I see where I've gotten "with the Spirit" and feel like I have an idea where I might be with Jesus. Now I have a problem; for my experience disagrees with the Word of God. When God and someone else disagree, then that someone else is wrong. Right now is one of those times we need to decide if we really believe what the Word says. Can we admit to ourselves that it really is better that Jesus went, which means what we have available now is much more than what was available when Jesus was here? Do our lives exhibit this? If not, we have no excuse, for the scripture is clear. The decision we need to make is what we will do about it. Will we stand upon the truth, believe, and fight for it? Or will we settle back into our life and hope it comes our way?

Always With Us

Let's start with some advantages to having the Spirit. John 14:16 tells us the Spirit will always be with us. Rather than having a physical manifestation that can only be in one place at a time, we have the Spirit of God dwelling inside of us. This same verse names Him as "The Helper," because He is willing and able to help us in our weakness, give guidance in our time of needs, and reveal truth us if we will listen. We have such a wonderful opportunity here that I believe we often overlook. As we walk through our day, especially in times of trouble, we should remember the Holy Spirit is inside us, willing and able to help.

> As for you, the anointing which you received from Him abides in you, and you have no need for anyone to teach you; but as His anointing teaches you about all things, and is true and is not a lie, and just as it has taught you, you abide in Him. — (1 John 2:27)

The Spirit can teach us all things, which leads us to a pivotal truth here that we need to grasp. We can study the Bible, take classes, go to seminaries, and read commentaries; nevertheless, truth comes from the Spirit. Remember what we learned from Peter's confession concerning Jesus; revelation comes from the Father. We can only understand so much on our own, but the Spirit gives us the revelation for us to grasp truth. Through Him, the truth can change our hearts.

Spirt Of Truth

> That is the Spirit of truth, whom the world cannot receive, because it does not see Him or know Him, but you know Him because He abides with you and will be in you. — (John 14:17)

The Spirit guides us into truth. Not only can this come by teaching us the truth, but also by bearing witness to the truth. If we will follow His leading, He will warn us about deception trying to sneak in upon us. Our enemy is cunning, especially with religious and legalistic spirits that mimic our faith, but the Holy Spirit can guard our path. I have already spoken on the Spirit's ability to bear witness to us in our hearts. He abides with us and in us, and we cannot be separated from Him. We can find faith knowing the Spirit is always there to guide us. Moreover, we are told that the Holy Spirit is the Spirit of truth. He is not revealing the truth as much as revealing God to us. To say it in a different manner, the Holy Spirit is here to reveal who God is, which just happens to be the greatest truth in this world.

> And bring to your remembrance all that I said to you. — (John 14:26)

As with so much of the Bible, we find ourselves back at Jesus. Jesus tells the disciples that the Holy Spirit was there to remind them of everything He had spoken to them. The Spirit will do this for us as well. He will bring to our remembrance the words of the Lord.

He reminds us of truth and gives us what we need to hear. Can you remember a time when the right scripture came into your mind when you needed it? Do you honestly believe that you are smart enough to pull that off on your own?

Convict

The next role of the Spirit is to convict us, but perhaps not necessarily as we have believed.

> And He, when He comes, will convict the world concerning sin and righteousness and judgment. — (John 16:8)

I love verses like these that get right down to the heart of the matter. Jesus is about to lay it out for us, so let's step through John 16:9-11 to understand the conviction of the Spirit.

> Concerning sin, because they do not believe in Me. — (John 16:9)

He convicts of sin, but did you catch why? We've been taught that it's the Holy Spirit condemning us of our sin. We do something wrong and feel condemned. We know we are worthless and always sinning, so we can't imagine why God would love us, much less use us. Surely that is the Spirit convicting us of our sinful nature. Or is it? According to this verse He convicts the world because of unbelief. The word used for the world is everyone, not just the unsaved. We often fall under a conviction of how awful we are and attribute that to the Spirit, but what if it wasn't the Holy Spirit convicting us? What if the sin that He convicts us of is not believing in Him? Perhaps He is not pointing out each sin, but rather that we have forgotten Christ in our lives.

> And concerning righteousness, because I go to the
> Father and you no longer see Me. — (John 16:10)

The Holy Spirit convicts us concerning the righteousness of Jesus. Since we cannot see Jesus upon the earth, the Spirit shows us what His righteousness is like. Perhaps He's not here to tell us how awful we are, but to show us how amazing our Lord is. He encourages us to be more. This is where we make the distinction. Conviction to live better, that's God. Condemnation about how bad we are, that's the devil. Don't listen to the condemnation. When you sin, you repent and take whatever steps you need to overcome, but then you move on. Letting condemnation come upon you will drag you down and make you useless. I've heard it said that living in condemnation is like sleeping with the enemy.

> And concerning judgment, because the ruler of this
> world has been judged. — (John 16:11)

We forget that judgement isn't necessarily a bad thing. It just depends upon what side of the ruling you find yourself. If you're on the right side, you will find all that has been taken from you restored. In fact, in the kingdom, we receive a greater portion back than what was taken. When judgment comes—if we are on the right side—we will find blessings. We know the devil has already been judged and it's only a matter of time until all is restored. I suspect we need to be reminded of this more than we realize, and that there is much to be restored to us if we will seek the righteous judge.

How Then Do We Receive?

> In Him, you also, after listening to the message
> of truth, the gospel of your salvation—having also
> believed, you were sealed in Him with the Holy Spirit
> of promise, who is given as a pledge of our inheritance,

> with a view to the redemption of God's own possession, to the praise of His glory. — (Ephesians 1:13-14)

Here is where our doctrines clash. We are all willing to say we need the Spirit, and we can all agree that having Him is better than having Jesus, but our paths often diverge at the implementation point. At salvation we can be sealed with the Holy Spirit. God has taken residence in us from this point, but there is much more.

The Filling

I have come to the point where I can no longer deny the truths put in front of me just because they make me uncomfortable. I have had pastors, family, friends, and teachers all with different viewpoints here. I've listened to ministers from multiple denominations and read many books. Though I've done all that, I will not stand upon another's view, but only upon the Word. Allow me to take you through the Word and make your own conclusions. I don't want to judge others for their belief, only to stand upon the truth itself.

> It happened that while Apollos was at Corinth, Paul passed through the upper country and came to Ephesus, and found some disciples. He said to them, "Did you receive the Holy Spirit when you believed?" And they said to him, "No, we have not even heard whether there is a Holy Spirit." And he said, "Into what then were you baptized?" And they said, "Into John's baptism." Paul said, "John baptized with the baptism of repentance, telling the people to believe in Him who was coming after him, that is, in Jesus." When they heard this, they were baptized in the name of the Lord Jesus. And when Paul had laid his hands upon them, the Holy Spirit came on them, and they began speaking with tongues and prophesying. — (Acts 9:1–6)

The Jesus We Forgot

Notice how the scripture says that Paul found disciples in Ephesus? This tells us something important we cannot overlook; these people were believers. These disciples had believed in God and had been baptized into repentance. According to Romans 10:9, if you confess and believe, you will be saved. Since these disciples were believers who had accepted salvation, how then were they missing the Holy Spirit? We can relate this to Acts 2, where the disciples were sent to await the Spirit in the upper room. Jesus had already told them they were clean, for they had believed and accepted Christ as their savior, yet there came another filling. After this filling, Peter spoke to the crowds and referenced Joel which said "in the last days I will pour forth of My spirit on all mankind" (Joel 2:28). Even John the Baptist discussed this filling.

> As for me, I baptize you with water for repentance, but He who is coming after me is mightier than I, and I am not fit to remove His sandals; He will baptize you with the Holy Spirit and fire. — (Matthew 3:11)

Stop for a minute and think, why did Jesus need to be baptized? Peter described John's baptism as the "baptism of repentance", but Jesus didn't need repentance. He was baptized into something else, in which we find the Spirit descending upon Him. Immediately, after this event, He left to be tempted and for the first time we see Him described as "Jesus, full of the Holy Spirit"(Luke 4:1). John's baptism was repentance which leads to Salvation, but Jesus baptism was that of the Spirit. Keep in mind, Jesus could not begin His ministry until He had been baptized with the Spirit.

> On one occasion, while he was eating with them, he gave them this command: "Do not leave Jerusalem, but wait for the gift my Father promised, which you have heard me speak about. For John baptized with water, but in a few days you will be baptized with the Holy Spirit. — (Acts 1:4–5)

These are the same disciples who had walked with Jesus for three years. They saw Him raise the dead, feed the hungry, heal the sick, cast out demons, and much more. Jesus had even sent them out to heal the sick, cast out devils, and proclaim the good news to many cities in Israel. Considering all this, let me ask you this. If the disciples who had been with Jesus needed to be filled with the Holy Spirit before they could begin their ministry, how much more do we need Him?

This is where I had to make a decision for myself. I have heard several different doctrines on the Holy Spirit, but it came down to which was greater, my doctrines or the God whom they serve? My comfort with what I had known wasn't important to God. He will move as He wishes, no matter if I agree with His methods. This is why I ask that you be open to what the Word says to you.

In my studies, I have come across stories of Christians in our day who have walked in a degree of power in God that reminds me of the original apostles. Some of these people have gone out to heal the sick in multitudes, even to the point where one city nearly closed down its hospitals. Others have been able to see a person for the first time and tell them their name, information about them, their problems, and the secrets in their hearts. Blind eyes are being opened, the dead raised, and cancers withered. I recently read of an Evangelist who went on a crusade and saw over one million people saved in single city. You may not have heard of these people, which only shows that we sometimes avoid the things we cannot explain. Yet, I can no longer ignore the truth that there is a separate experience of God apart from baptism. The disciples found it at Pentecost. Cornelius and His family had the Spirit fall upon them while listening to Paul. Let's look at what happened when Peter and John went to Samaria

> Now when the apostles in Jerusalem heard that Samaria had received the word of God, they sent them Peter and John, who came down and prayed for them that they might receive the Holy Spirit. For He had not yet fallen upon any of them; they had simply

> been baptized in the name of the Lord Jesus. Then they began laying their hands on them, and they were receiving the Holy Spirit. — (Acts 8:14–17)

The people of Samaria had received the word and again I can't find any way to pretend as if they were not saved. Yet, the Holy Spirit had not fallen upon them. Again, we find salvation and the Holy Spirit not linked together. I've listened to a pastor try to explain this away as just something strange God did for a while and that the Spirit wasn't being poured out to the believers for a short while. If that were the case, why? Why would God change that? If so, there must be a reason. In this pastor's desire to explain this away, he overlooked what I found as the most important part of this story. For a clearer example of what he overlooked, let's look at a similar story regarding Peter in Acts 10.

> While Peter was still speaking these words, the Holy Spirit fell upon all those who were listening to the message. All the circumcised believers who came with Peter were amazed, because the gift of the Holy Spirit had been poured out on the Gentiles also. For they were hearing them speaking with tongues and exalting God. Then Peter answered, "Surely no one can refuse the water for these to be baptized who have received the Holy Spirit just as we did, can he?" And he ordered them to be baptized in the name of Jesus Christ. — (Acts 10:44–48)

Here's the observation that I cannot move past. In each passage I've mentioned, the apostles knew when the Holy Spirit was poured out upon other believers. Think about it, in this particular scripture the new believers were baptized in water after the Holy Spirit fell upon them. What does this tell you? First, that the baptism of water is something done after salvation and is not itself a part of salvation. More importantly, the baptism of the Spirit was immediately evident.

This isn't an internal change that slowly becomes clear as we see a life changed. It was immediate and obvious. When the Holy Spirit came upon them, things happened. There was no question.

> But you will receive power when the Holy Spirit has come upon you. — (Acts 1:8)

The real power in our walk comes when the Spirit has come upon us. The baptism of the Spirit is not necessary for salvation. It is also not necessary to love God or even hear from God. It is necessary to walk in power and change the world. Remember, Jesus wouldn't let the disciples out until they had been baptized in the Spirit. We need the Spirit. I'm not talking about a "we know He's around and sometimes talks to us" relationship. Nor do we just need to be sealed by the Spirit at salvation that we may know we are saved. We need the power of the Spirit working in our lives if we're to reach this world. The apostles spread the good news across the known world in a couple decades. Yet even with all the resources we have available, it feels like we make so little progress in our age.

A Willing Father

> If you then, being evil, know how to give good gifts to your children, how much more will your heavenly Father give the Holy Spirit to those who ask Him? — (Luke 11:13)

God desires to give us the Spirit. Jesus compared our desire to give good things to our children with God's desire to provide the Spirit to His. What does that mean? It means that God truly delights in providing the Spirit to us. I love to give my daughter gifts. The joy she shows at such a little thing would make me do it all over again. She's my daughter, and I will often pass up on things I want to provide things she desires. If I, a sinful man, can treat my daughter this way, how much more our Father in heaven. Furthermore, His willingness also means that the Spirit is the best gift God can give to us. It is perhaps the thing we need the most.

How To Receive

I do not feel that I am a good authority in this area unfortunately, as I don't have a lot of experience with others here. Having said that, I would start with belief. Read the word until you are convinced in your heart that the baptism of the Spirit is something real that you not only need but cannot do your work without. If you don't believe this is real and crucial, then don't move ahead with it until you do. I suggest you wait until your heart and spirit have convinced you. Next, you ask just like the verse says. Pray to your Father who gives good gifts and ask for the Spirit. Nothing fancy, come on your knees and keep coming until you get it. From the scriptures you may notice that in many cases the Spirit came after the apostles laid their hands upon someone. The laying on of hands facilitates an impartation of the Spirit, power, or authority onto a person. You can find this in the Old Testament and the New. It doesn't have to be this way, but often it is. If you have a pastor or mature Christian with experience here, go to them and they can help guild you. Unfortunately, in some parts of the body, you may not have access to someone to discuss this with. Do not worry. There are people around who have this experience, but sometimes they keep it quiet because some things just aren't accepted in parts of the church. God is a good Father and will provide all that you need when you need it. Trust in Him and do not give up.

Being Filled With God

> For this reason I bow my knees before the Father, from whom every family in heaven and on earth derives its name, that He would grant you, according to the riches of His glory, to be strengthened with power through His Spirit in the inner man, so that Christ may dwell in your hearts through faith; and

> that you, being rooted and grounded in love, may be able to comprehend with all the saints what is the breadth and length and height and depth, and to know the love of Christ which surpasses knowledge, that you may be filled up to all the fullness of God.
> — (Ephesians 3:14–19)

Paul prays that we would be strengthened by God's Spirit in our inner man. That Christ may dwell in our hearts, and that we would be grounded in His love. Next, he tells us why we should be grounded in this love—"to know the love of Christ which surpasses knowledge, that you may be filled up to all the fullness of God." Two big points here. First, we should know the love that surpasses knowledge. That means this isn't just a knowing with our minds, instead it's an experiential knowledge which lives down in our heart and spirit. Second, the reason you need to know the love of Christ is "that you may be filled up to all the fullness of God." In order to be filled in our spirit with God, we must understand the love of Christ. Typically, we think this is done through purity, selfless acts, or piety, but it isn't. It's understanding the love of Christ which will fill us with God. For this reason, meditate upon His love. Read upon it. Spend time feeling His love, imagining it, and talking with Him about it. The Spirit will not work apart from love.

Praying In The Spirit

> For if I pray in a tongue, my spirit prays, but my mind is unfruitful. What is the outcome then? I will pray with the spirit and I will pray with the mind also; I will sing with the spirit and I will sing with the mind also. Otherwise if you bless in the spirit only, how will the one who fills the place of the ungifted say the "Amen" at your giving of thanks, since he does not know what you are saying? For you are giving thanks well enough, but the other person is not edified. I

thank God, I speak in tongues more than you all. — (1 Corinthians 14:14–18)

Well, now I've up and done it.

Not only did I talk about the baptism of the Spirit, but now I'm talking about tongues. How many more toes can I step on. Fortunately—or unfortunately depending upon how you look upon it—I will not overlook truth even if it's uncomfortable or looked down upon by another. I may keep it to myself, but I won't set it aside. In this passage, Paul is talking about tongues and praying in the spirit. Even though he is talking about how it is more desirable to talk to others where they can understand us (not tongues), that in no way diminishes praying in the spirit. Paul has made a connection here between tongues and praying in the spirit so that we can understand that he is talking about praying in tongues. Notice he says, "I thank God, I speak in tongues more than you all"? Why would he say that if tongues weren't beneficial? He's thankful that he speaks in tongues more than everyone else because of the good it does. If we back up a little in the chapter we find this verse.

One who speaks in a tongue edifies himself. — (1 Corinthians 14:4)

One of the types of tongues, which is distinct from the gift of tongues, is praying in the Spirit. That type of prayer edifies ourselves because it is our spirit praying. Our spirit knows what to pray when our mind doesn't. As we pray in tongues, we pray in God's will, though we don't even know what we pray. Paul was thankful that he did it more than the rest. Many try to avoid tongues as it is an uncomfortable concept in many of our churches, but do we not look at Paul as an example for us? Should this not provoke us to want to do it for ourselves? I wish I could give you all the benefits of praying in the spirit, but I can't. Again, feel free to go find other books or people to go over. What I'm here to do is to open you up to what God has provided in the Spirit that we need to accomplish His purposes.

Why would He create something so strange as praying in tongues? I cannot give a good answer, but I do know this:

> But God chose the foolish things of the world to shame the wise — (1 Corinthians 1:27)

The Gifts

Now let's also discuss the gifts. This will not be an in-depth analysis, more of a quick overview. As part of a men's group I was involved with, I have taken a spiritual gifts test several times. If you haven't seen one of these, think of it as a personality test, but about the gifts of the Spirit. It basically gauges how you lean toward different "gifts" and then judges you on a point system to see where you're more inclined. The basis I was given for this method is that at salvation God gives us each a gift, and the test is used to help you get an indication regarding which gift you have. Unfortunately, this explanation just doesn't work for me. I don't like contradicting people, I really don't, but that's the truth. Here's the verse that gets many people confused.

> As each has received a gift, use it to serve one another, as good stewards of God's varied grace. — (1 Peter 4:10)

At first glance, the verse seems pretty clear. Each one of us has received a gift, and we should use that for the church. In actuality, the translation leans more toward "each one who has received a gift." It doesn't say one or only one gift. On top of this, the word isn't actually a "gift", but a "deposit of grace". Basically, whatever deposits God has made into your life, use them to serve others. If He gives you a spiritual gift, use that. If He's provided you with more money than others, use that as well.

When we speak of spiritual gifts, there are at least three categories I've found. First, we have what can be called the ministry gifts.

> But to each one of us grace was given according to the measure of Christ's gift. Therefore it says, "When He ascended on high, He led captive a host of captives, And He gave gifts to men." (Now this expression, "He ascended," what does it mean except that He also had descended into the lower parts of the earth? He who descended is Himself also He who ascended far above all the heavens, so that He might fill all things.) And He gave some as apostles, and some as prophets, and some as evangelists, and some as pastors and teachers, for the equipping of the saints for the work of service, to the building up of the body of Christ — (Ephesians 4:7–12)

You might also hear this set of gifts referred to as the "five-fold ministry." These are the ministry gifts given by Christ to the church to build her up. If you go and look, the word gift here is a different word in the Greek than the last passage. In this case the gift isn't a gift to the person, but the person is the gift to the church. We need these offices restored to our churches to build up the people in the kingdom. The next set of gifts are from God.

> And God has appointed in the church, first apostles, second prophets, third teachers, then miracles, then gifts of healings, helps, administrations, various kinds of tongues. — (1 Corinthians 12:28)

There's an overlap here. Why? I can't tell you, I only know in part. Like I said, I wasn't planning to really go into depth here. To me these seem more like our services. Perhaps it's a gifting of how you serve the rest of the body. Maybe we do receive this at salvation, maybe not. I haven't received a revelation in this and that's ok. It is perfectly acceptable to not have answers. A few more gifts that seem very similar are listed in the passage below.

> Since we have gifts that differ according to the grace given to us, each of us is to exercise them accordingly: if prophecy, according to the proportion of his faith; if service, in his serving; or he who teaches, in his teaching; or he who exhorts, in his exhortation; he who gives, with liberality; he who leads, with diligence; he who shows mercy, with cheerfulness.
> — (Romans 12:6–8)

Then we come to the gifts given by the Holy Spirit.

> But to each one is given the manifestation of the Spirit for the common good. For to one is given the word of wisdom through the Spirit, and to another the word of knowledge according to the same Spirit; to another faith by the same Spirit, and to another gifts of healing by the one Spirit, and to another the effecting of miracles, and to another prophecy, and to another the distinguishing of spirits, to another various kinds of tongues, and to another the interpretation of tongues. But one and the same Spirit works all these things, distributing to each one individually just as He wills.
> — (1 Corinthians 12:7–11)

There are nine gifts of the Holy Spirit, given out "as He wills." One interpretation again could be that each of us gets a gift, but you will find several scriptures (mainly in Acts) referencing gifts that believers received after salvation. You can also find believers (especially the apostles) who walked in several of the gifts. It's the verse at the end of this chapter which convinces me that we can have more than one gift.

> But earnestly desire the greater gifts. — (1 Corinthians 12:31)

If we had only one gift, why would we pursue the greater ones? Not only are we told to desire and pursue the gifts, we are told to pursue multiple gifts. What this tells me is that after we have received the Spirit, which was often followed by the speaking in tongues or prophecy in Acts, we should then desire spiritual gifts such that we may use them to serve others.

One of my fears is to come up to heaven and see a table laid out with everything God provided for me, only to realize I used a tiny fraction because I wasn't willing to believe. Pursue the gifts. Ask God and desire them. Again, sometimes they are received from someone who has the gift laying their hands upon another believer and asking God. They can be imparted just Timothy's gift was imparted at the laying on of hands. Other times, it's straight from God. Do not give up in your search. We miss out on so much because we don't want it enough to show God we would appreciate it. Remember the lesson of Esau.

> See to it that no one comes short of the grace of God; that no root of bitterness springing up causes trouble, and by it many be defiled; That there be no immoral or godless person like Esau, who sold his own birthright for a single meal. For you know that even afterwards, when he desired to inherit the blessing, he was rejected, for he found no place for repentance, though he sought for it with tears. — (Hebrews 12:15–17)

Esau had a birthright, a gift from God that he so casually put aside for his own comfort. Jesus has paid a high price for our inheritance, do not set it aside so easily.

Count the Cost

One of the unfortunate but consistent truths I have found in my life is that the biggest hinderance in my relationship with God is myself. God has taught me much and revealed many truths which I could be walking in, yet I walk in so little. As I've mentioned before, a saying worth repeating is "we are as close to God as we choose to be." I suspect that many of us fall into this category. Given that, I have two questions for us.

What are we afraid of?

Why do we hold back?

We skirt along the edges of God's glory, but hold onto this world. We see where God is, but we are not willing to sacrifice ourselves to reach there. Are we afraid that we might actually find God? Perhaps we know enough to realize that He might come in and push aside everything we hold of value to lead us down His path. Perhaps we are afraid that we may lose ourselves in Him. Yet, why not give in? Why not sacrifice? How is it that we can continually take so little when God has prepared so much for us? Think about it. He is God. Repeat that.... He IS God. Yet we are content to settle with our petty theological discussions and our goose bumps on Sundays. In our "fellowship" gatherings and social-click small groups, we've settled for our cultivated Christianity and our schedules for God rather than the God behind them.

What has happened to us?

How did God become like a school course where we expect to confine Him to our schedule and our desires? Do we think God will be content in the schedules of our Sunday schools, quiet times, and worship services while we continue to live life in our own way? Or do we expect him to invade our very lives? Do we expect Him to push out all we have that draws us away from Him and show us just how big He is? It's not going to feel good and we will be uncomfortable and unsure, but that is because our logic is backwards. To live, we must die. That is how God works. Why? I don't know, but because of sin, God requires death for life. As such, we follow Christ's example. What do we have to lose? This world. And what do we have to gain? Eternity.

> We have been buried with Him through baptism into death — (Romans 6:4)

It's your choice.

> For whoever wishes to save his life will lose it; but whoever loses his life for My sake will find it. — (Matthew 16:25)

I have a little secret for you. It seems so very obvious to me, and yet it also looks like so few realize it. This life is not about you. This is the secret that will help you to make that step. Once you really understand that this life is about God and not you, then there's no issue giving up your desires. You will actually be doing what makes more sense. Why spend time glorifying your life that is so fleeting; instead, give glory to the One who is forever.

> As for man, his days are like grass; as a flower of the field, so he flourishes. When the wind has passed over it, it is no more, and its place acknowledges it no longer. — (Psalm 103:15–16)

At this point in the book, my prayer for you is that you've come to that place where knowing God becomes the sole desire of your heart. You can continue on with the book, but know that until you can come to this place where you're willing to surrender, you can only go so far in God. I believe the Word is pretty clear on that. Now you must come full circle back to the beginning. God is everything. If your heart is to please him, then we must follow the One whom we know pleased Him upon this earth.

Cost For Disciples

Let us look back to Jesus. Always back to Him. He paid the price to give us our lives back; who better to show us the way. We must understand that there is a cost to following Christ. Look at some examples from those who wanted to follow Him.

- Peter and Andrew left their fishing jobs to follow. — (Matthew 3:19)
- James and John left their father and the family business to follow. — (Mark 1:19)
- Matthew left everything behind at his tax collector's booth to follow. — (Luke 5:28)
- To the scribe who asked to follow, Jesus replied: "The foxes have holes and the birds of the air have nests, but the Son of Man has nowhere to lay His head." — (Matthew 8:20)
- Another disciple asked to go and bury his father, Jesus replied: "Follow Me, and allow the dead to bury their own dead." — (Matthew 8:22)
- To the rich young ruler, Jesus said: "One thing you lack: go and sell all you possess and give to the poor, and you will have treasure in heaven; and come, follow Me." — (Mark 10:21)
- "Another also said, 'I will follow You, Lord; but first permit me to say good-bye to those at home.' But Jesus said to him, 'No one, after putting his hand to the plow and looking back is fit for the kingdom of God.'" — (Luke 9:61–62)

Have you been required to leave things behind? It is different for everyone. Sometimes it's a slow progression, and other times it's immediate. Not all are called to leave family or possessions. Each person is called as God sees fit.

Follower Versus Disciple

Too often we desire the salvation and gifts from God, but we don't want the cost of developing a relationship with Him. I believe this cost is the dividing line between a believer in Jesus and a disciple of Jesus. While Jesus was walking the earth, He would often have large crowds of people following. You can easily imagine how this would happen as He went around feeding the crowds and healing the sick. Some ministers would have relished this, but it's as if Jesus didn't want the large crowds. We can find him occasionally turning to the crowds and doing something like this.

> Now large crowds were going along with Him; and He turned and said to them, "If anyone comes to Me, and does not hate his own father and mother and wife and children and brothers and sisters, yes, and even his own life, he cannot be My disciple. Whoever does not carry his own cross and come after Me cannot be My disciple. For which one of you, when he wants to build a tower, does not first sit down and calculate the cost to see if he has enough to complete it? Otherwise, when he has laid a foundation and is not able to finish, all who observe it begin to ridicule him, saying, 'This man began to build and was not able to finish.' Or what king, when he sets out to meet another king in battle, will not first sit down and consider whether he is strong enough with ten thousand men to encounter the one coming against him with twenty thousand? Or else, while the other is still far away, he sends a delegation and asks for terms of peace. So then, none of you can be My disciple who does not give up all his own possessions. Therefore, salt is good; but if even salt has become tasteless, with what will it be seasoned? It is useless either for the soil or for the manure pile; it is thrown out. He who has ears to hear, let him hear." — (Luke 14:25–35)

Jesus was clear with them. If you want to follow me, there's a cost.

Often when He spoke like this, the crowds would leave. If you really wish to become a disciple of Jesus, to learn from Him and come to know Him intimately, Jesus said there is a cost to be paid. When the moment comes that Jesus says to you "follow me", will you be ready to pay the price?

> Do not think that I came to bring peace on the earth; I did not come to bring peace, but a sword. For I came to set a man against his father, and a daughter against her mother, and a daughter-in-law against her mother-in-law; and a man's enemies will be the members of his household. He who loves father or mother more than Me is not worthy of Me; and he who loves son or daughter more than Me is not worthy of Me. And he who does not take his cross and follow after Me is not worthy of Me. He who has found his life will lose it, and he who has lost his life for My sake will find it. — (Matthew 10:34–39)

Jesus is not convenient. I've said it before and will continue to say. He is not for the faint of heart; instead, He is for those who recognize truth and are brave enough to stand for it.

The Cost

Let's take a look at this cost.

> If anyone would come after me, he must deny himself, and take up his cross daily and follow me. — (Luke 9:23)

One day the Lord pointed out to me something that I had never considered before in this verse. After all these years I assumed I had the basics down, but what He pointed out to me was His use of the cross in these verses. I never considered that Jesus mentioned this to His disciples before He died. For us, the cross symbolizes salvation and grace, but when the disciples saw a cross, they thought of capital punishment. The cross was where the worst criminals went to their death. For the disciples, taking up their cross would mean that final journey the criminal takes to his execution. The most current representation of this I can think of is from the book, "The Green Mile." The green mile was the last "mile" the convict would walk from his cell to the execution chamber. To take up the cross would be to acknowledge your death. As the criminal did this, he couldn't help but understand that he no longer had a choice over his life and it was now forfeit. No matter what choices he makes at this point, his life was about to end. He would take up the cross that was to be His death, and he would walk to the place where he would die with the crowds gathered to watch him go.

Can you imagine it? Can you imagine picking up this wood that would soon be the end of your life and carrying it up to Golgotha; only to lay it down, be nailed to it, and die. There's no nice way to describe crucifixion. It was a statement to all of the judgment against you. More than just death, it was a statement of condemnation from the world. In this context, what does taking up your cross mean? Since this was before anyone knew to associate Jesus's death to the cross, we can assume that Jesus was telling those that followed Him that they must be willing to give up their right to life to follow. As He said:

> For whoever wishes to save his life will lose it, but whoever loses his life for My sake will find it. — (Matthew 16:25)

Although they couldn't understand the full truth of this without His death, they could understand that to take up the cross would be to admit to themselves that their lives were forfeit. To follow Jesus was to give up all they had. The cross to us is a symbol of hope, but to them it was a symbol of despair. It's like one of us saying, go sit in the electric chair and strap in. This wasn't an uplifting statement; it was just true. We often look at this statement as denying ourselves, but I think it's more. Jesus was asking, "are you ready to die for me?" I imagine Jesus reminded them of this during the forty days after His resurrection He spent with them before ascending to heaven. Suddenly the fear from these words of Jesus could take on a new meaning. It wasn't just a statement of death. Paul put it this way:

> I have been crucified with Christ; and it is no longer I who live, but Christ lives in me; and the life which I now live in the flesh I live by faith in the Son of God, who loved me and give Himself up for me. — (Galatians 2:20)

For Paul, taking up the cross meant putting to death the old self, so that Christ may live through him. Not only does this mean to crucify my old desires of sin, but my own desire of the law. If you read through the rest of Galatians 2, you'll see this. We have to put aside what we think we must do to be saved. Our good motives can stand between us and God if we believe they are what will save us. No, it's only through grace we are saved and only through grace that we can live for Him. We live by that faith, and anything we do from now on must be based on that, not on our attempts of righteous. Our lives can be resurrected from the dead, the sinful life we lay down, as Christ lives through us instead. A glorious life can be found.

Count The Cost

> For which one of you, when he wants to build a tower, does not first sit down and calculate the cost to see if he has enough to complete it? Otherwise, when he has laid a foundation and is not able to finish, all who observe it begin to ridicule him, saying, 'This man began to build and was not able to finish. Or what king, when he sets out to meet another king in battle, will not first sit down and consider whether he

is strong enough with ten thousand men to encounter the one coming against him with twenty thousand? Or else, while the other is still far away, he sends a delegation and asks for terms of peace. So then, none of you can be My disciple who does not give up all his own possessions. — (Luke 14:28–33)

God has really impressed me with this scripture in my walk recently. For weeks, I had the words "count the cost" burned into my thoughts. It's easy to tell ourselves there is a cost, but much harder to try and calculate what it might be. After this went on for a while, I decided to start listing things out. I began to write out the costs of following Jesus. I had a column of the things I would need to give up. The most obvious things were sin. Sin can be enjoyable, sin can be comforting, sin can build up our pride, but these things must be given up. I realized I must rely upon God to fill the void that these things will leave behind. The next part I found was my priorities. I had certain things which had taken priority over God. These aren't open sins, for often they can be good things, but by putting them before the Lord they were hindering me. Examples for me were things like TV shows, books, and even some parts of my family life. For example, I wanted to please my wife more than I wanted to please God. In this I might compromise my relationship with God to do what I thought was easier for my relationship with her. As I looked at all the areas that would cost me, I found myself a bit overwhelmed to say the least.

Don't fear. Sometimes we'll hear something like this and quickly shut down because we know we can't live up to the standard. God does not expect you to be ready to give it all up immediately. In fact, I don't know that making a list was even a good idea. When we are a new Christian, we don't even understand what all this could mean. God gives us grace for what we need. Look back to the offerings in the Old Testament. There were several types of offerings given in the Levitical law. The first offering listed was the burnt offering. It was an offering to acknowledge the Lord for who He is, and to show our devotion to Him.

> Speak to the sons of Israel and say to them, 'When any man of you brings an offering to the Lord, you shall bring your offering of animals from the herd or the flock. If his offering is a burnt offering from the herd, he shall offer it, a male without defect; he shall offer it at the doorway of the tent of meeting, that he may be accepted before the Lord… But if his offering is from the flock, of the sheep or of the goats, for a burnt offering, he shall offer it a male without defect… 'But if his offering to the Lord is a burnt offering of birds, then he shall bring his offering from the turtledoves or from young pigeons. — (Leviticus 1:2–3,10,14)

Notice there were three different offerings that were acceptable here: a bull, a sheep, and a bird. Three levels of sacrifice were acceptable to the Lord. The lowest was a pigeon or turtledove.

> The priest shall bring it to the altar, and wring off its head and offer it up in smoke on the altar; and its blood is to be drained out on the side of the altar. He shall also take away its crop with its feathers and cast it beside the altar eastward, to the place of the ashes. Then he shall tear it by its wings, but shall not sever it. And the priest shall offer it up in smoke on the altar on the wood which is on the fire; it is a burnt offering, an offering by fire of a soothing aroma to the Lord — (Leviticus 1:15–17)

Offering can be messy. In our case, we're offering up part of our lives, so we will be removing something—often something we're attached to. The pigeon was the least costly and typically the first step in our journey. At salvation, we offer our lives to Jesus even though we understand little of what that means. The head is removed because we have a new head, and we follow where He leads. The feathers are removed. Our appearance doesn't help us, for we have not chosen Him for what others think. We'll probably look foolish to them. The wings—our strength in ourselves— are broken, but nothing else is cut off. We offer our whole self to the Lord. Later as we grow in our walk, the Lord will ask for more. One day He'll begin asking for a sheep.

> He shall slay it on the side of the altar northward before the Lord, and Aaron's sons the priests shall sprinkle its blood around on the altar. He shall then cut it into its pieces with its head and its fat, and the priest shall arrange them on the wood which is on the fire that is on the altar. The entrails, however, and the legs he shall wash with water. And the priest shall offer all of it, and offer it up in smoke on the altar; it is a burnt offering, an offering by fire of a soothing aroma to the Lord. — (Leviticus 1:11–13)

The cost increases, a pigeon to a sheep to a bull. Each level will take more of us. Again, the offering had parts. The head first, for our mind is one of the greatest creations of God, but also the area that needs the most control. The fat in the Old Testament spoke of strength. People who were able to gain fat in those times were either the strong or the rich. Our strength and our success must be offered unto Him. The word "entrails" is the word that means the innards— the inmost part of the body. This is where the Hebrews believed the emotions and desires came from. We offer God our dreams, our desires, and our emotions. The legs are what take us along our path. We must offer our journey and our future to the God who has placed it before us.

This is a journey. We cannot come before the Lord and try to jump straight to the end. We start with the small offering. Then when we're ready, God will step in and say, "I want that." Most of us make it a little way along this journey, until He gets to something too costly for us to let go. At that point, we get stuck. We don't give up what He knows we need to, and then we wonder why we go years without feeling like anything has changed. Remember, the burnt offering is not about our sin. There is another offering in the Old Testament that is the trespass offering which was given when you have sinned against the Lord. The burnt offering is about devotion. Living under the new covenant, we no longer offer animals as sacrifices, but that doesn't mean the offerings have gone away. The offering itself still exists and is symbolic in our lives. The burnt offering ties into our love for God. Today He may be asking you to give up a little sleep to find a quiet time with Him. As a new father, early morning and late night are the prime times. I have freedom then to choose, and God wants some of that time from me, not my left overs. This book is also a sacrifice to Him. As I spend time writing, I know this time is spent for Him, and not myself. Who am I to think I have something for the world? I want to glorify Him and bless Him by helping someone else. Maybe He's asking you to give up some music. There have been certain songs I've had to delete because they were filling my mind with junk where God wanted it consecrated for Him. Or perhaps a show that's taking too strong a place. A job that drives you from Him. A mind that is full of fiction and not the truth. There's so many areas that steal away our affections and our time.

The Cost Is High

If you truly wish to be a disciple of Christ, to follow Him with your heart, you must count the cost. What in your life needs to fall second to Him? What parts of the world do you love more than your love for God and His glory? This isn't choosing specific things but a whole change in our mindset. There's a song by Rich Mullins where the chorus says, "but the world can't stand what it cannot own and it can't own You cause You did not have a home." Jesus home was not here on earth. There's nothing wrong with enjoying the things in this world, but there's a problem when we love the creation more than the creator. Jesus said that if someone does not hate his mother and brothers, he is not worthy. The cost of discipleship is high, for it is our very lives.

> If your right eye makes you stumble, tear it out and throw it from you; for it is better for you to lose one of the parts of your body, than for your whole body to be thrown into hell. If your right hand makes you stumble, cut it off and throw it from you; for it is better for you to lose one of the parts of your body, than for your whole body to go into hell. — (Matthew 5:29–30)

Is Jesus telling us to tear out our eye if it is making us sin? Actually, yes. I'm not going to take this too literally and starting cutting off parts of my body, but that is what Jesus said. He was so serious about our relationship, that to Him this was a worthwhile cost. Remember, Jesus had that point of view we have so much trouble with. Often His words were confusing because to Him the spiritual was more real than the physical. So you must ask yourself, is your life with God more important than your life on earth?

I've been married for a while now. On several occasions I've found myself in a position where my job was causing friction in my marriage. At these points I would weigh the costs of things and seriously consider whether the job was worth it. If it was causing too many problems, perhaps I should be looking for a new job, because I knew my marriage was more important than my job. How much more the Lord? If our job keeps us too busy to spend time with Him, perhaps it's best to look for another. If a relationship we have is crowding God out, then that's one relationship we can do without. If you wish to follow Jesus, He must be the top priority. Anything that comes in the way needs to be dealt with.

I'm not saying you should give up your families, your career, or even things that you enjoy. God delights in blessing us. He is our

Father after all, and who hasn't seen the joy of a father giving gifts to their children. Most of this comes down to priorities. Give God the first fruits, make sure you've done what is pleasing to Him, then He'll lead you to things that please you. After you've done what needs to be done for the day and know you have honored Him, then relax and enjoy yourself, but keep listening. Always be ready to hear from Him. As you begin to walk more with God in mind, He'll begin to speak more to you of things He'd like, of ways you can be a blessing to Him and others.

A piece of advice; don't go looking for everything that could be impacting you. If you start trying to clean out your life yourself, the devil will be happy to help out. He'll start pointing out things and giving you reasons they're bad when they aren't. He will put a legalistic spirit over your life until you "strain out a gnat but swallow a camel" (Matthew 23:24). Wait for the Lord. If you see an obvious sin in your life, it's clear God doesn't want that. Past that, wait for the Lord to impress you that something has become more important than Him before pulling it out. I've made the mistake of taking on too many areas I thought I should and never fully dealing with any of them. Take care that you listen and act though. I suspect most of us have at least one area we know the Lord has been speaking to us about where we haven't yet responded in obedience.

Our relationship with God is limited by our actions. God will bring things up that He wants us to put on the altar. Often, it's a habitual sin we have. Maybe it's lust or pride. Maybe we drink too much, or eat more than we should. God is gracious, but there can be limits. He will remind you, and if you don't fix it, He'll come back to it again. If God has brought something to you that you need to place upon that altar, there is a reason. Your growth with Him will often be stuck until you overcome that particular issue. How many Christians have you heard that seem to be in the same place so much of their lives. They're praying the same prayers for strength and help, but never seem to move on in success. I've been there myself. I have gone back into some journal entries I wrote two decades ago, and feel like I've not really grown at all. That's because I was struggling with the same failures in the past that I was still doing at the time. I hadn't given up that area to the Lord and moved on with Him. I know more of the Bible, I have more experience and understanding, but my relationship with the Lord hadn't changed much. I suspect this is why so many in the church don't feel like God is speaking to them. He has in fact already spoken to them and they didn't respond. After a while, they grew numb to His words, not realizing that they were drowning out the very God they serve. You want an example of this, look to Bethsaida. They had Jesus come and work many miracles among them. You would think they would then have this major change in the town, yet Jesus later rebuked them saying:

> Woe to you, Chorazin! Woe to you, Bethsaida! For if the miracles that were performed in you had been performed in Tyre and Sidon, they would have repented long ago in sackcloth and ashes. — (Matthew 11:21)

This is the same place that Jesus took the blind man out of town to heal him, then told him not to go back into town. His physical blindness was a representation of what happened to the whole town. God had come and moved among them. He called for them, but they stopped listening. Because of this a spiritual blindness and deafness had come over them. It was dangerous enough that Jesus didn't want this man to go back or he might lose his sight again, physically and spiritually.

A Step Beyond

When Old Testament Israel would return and recommit themselves to the Lord, they would offer a sacrifice. For example, when Solomon dedicated the temple to the Lord, they sacrificed thousands of animals upon the altar. It wasn't until the sacrifices were done that the presence of the Lord came down and filled the temple. Though we don't sacrifice animals anymore, those sacrifices were always just a replacement for the true spiritual action.

> Therefore I urge you, brethren, by the mercies of God, to present your bodies a living and holy sacrifice, acceptable to God, which is your spiritual service of worship. — (Romans 12:1)

God responds to the sacrifices of His people. There is something about sacrifice that draws Him near. Further, there is also a commitment past our salvation that can be made to the Lord. A commitment that is necessary for our intimacy with the Lord. The early apostles recognized this and spoke of it. You've seen it written at the beginning of many of their letters.

> James, a bond-servant of God and of the Lord Jesus Christ. — (James 1:1)

> Paul, a bond-servant of Christ Jesus. — (Romans 1:1)

> Simon Peter, a bond-servant and apostle of Jesus Christ. — (2 Peter 1:1)

Bond-servant.

There exists a bond-servant commitment that we can make with the Lord to show our dedication and service toward Him. It's something that shows more than a general trust and faith in Him to save us. Mary understood this as Gabriel told her she was to bear Jesus. Imagine with me; Mary is engaged, and it seems her life is on track. If this was our day, she probably had the dress picked out, the announcements sent, and the reception planned. The plans were made and she was just waiting for everything to happen. Then an angel shows up and tells her that she's going to have a child, but not by her fiancé. Also, that other little detail where her child was to be a king. Do you think that fit into her plans? Even more, don't you think she would expect to be sent away from Joseph, for having a child that wasn't his? Instead of fear or denial, look at her response:

> And Mary said, "Behold, the bondslave of the Lord; may it be done to me according to your word." And the angel departed from her. — (Luke 1:38)

She accepted her place just like that. What I suspect we missed in her past was the moment where her relationship with God grew to the point she gave Him complete access and trust. Her response was more like an after-thought. She had placed her life before the Lord to use as He wills. To understand what a bond-servant is, we must look back to the Old Testament to find out.

> If you buy a Hebrew servant, he is to serve you for six years. But in the seventh year, he shall go free, without paying anything. If he comes alone, he is to go free alone; but if he has a wife when he comes, she is to go with him. If his master gives him a wife and she bears him sons or daughters, the woman and her children shall belong to her master, and only the man shall go free. But if the servant declares, 'I love my master and my wife and children and do not want to go free,' then his master must take him before the judges. He shall take him to the door or the doorpost and pierce his ear with an awl. Then he will be his servant for life. — (Exodus 21:2–6)

There were servants, then there were bond-servants. The servants were bought by the master, but were to be freed in the seventh year to avoid perpetual slavery in Israel. However, after six years, if the servant desired it they could choose to stay with their master. This choice was not temporary. If a servant made this choice, it was for life. They were choosing to give away any chance at freedom. Since this was a serious decision, they were taken before the judges as a witness and then they were marked. A hole was punched through their ear to identify their choice. In this way, everyone would know they belonged to someone.

As a Christian, God has bought us with a price. For a period of time, we are the servant. We've been bought and we try our best to do what our master says. But then a time comes where we can make another choice. It's not that salvation ends, but that something greater can begin. We can choose to give up our desires, our choices, and our future to our master. This isn't a light-hearted decision. This is a decision that says from now on I will do whatever you ask. I will serve you for the rest of my life. I give up what I could be, to be what I can for you. As servants we love our salvation, but often we still love many other parts of our lives. We're not willing to give them up to the Lord, because we want to have both. We think we can control those areas of our lives and still serve the Lord with what's left. You can do this, but you'll never reach your potential in this way. You'll either become more frustrated with your life, or become callous and miss out on what God is doing. We need the time to come to know the Lord and see what our life could be with Him, then we can make the choice to be fully His. He comes and marks us as His own servant and we give up our futures to forever be at His call. This may seem like a one-way commitment, but it isn't. In the Old Testament, it was the bond-servants that were the most trusted and closest to their master. For example, do you remember the servant Abraham sent to find a wife for Isaac? If you look at the Hebrew, you'll find it wasn't a servant, but his bond-servant. Because of their choices, the bond-servants could be entrusted with more. As part of this same agreement, the master committed to always care for that servant for the rest of their life. It was a two-way commitment that made them a part of the family.

Challenge

So where do you start? It's easy to say things, but much harder to actually start doing something. How about a challenge? Tomorrow morning when you wake up, I want you to remember this chapter. In particular, I want you to remember Luke 9:23.

> If anyone would come after me, he must deny himself, and take up his cross daily and follow me. — (Luke 9:23)

Bring it to God and talk to Him about it. My challenge is to commit tomorrow to Him. That's one nice thing about our life, it's full of tomorrows. Remember what the verse says, "take up your cross daily." I challenge you to take up your cross tomorrow. I'm not asking you to commit your whole life to always take up your cross, that's too big for most of us to commit and be able to follow through without time dedicated preparing us for it. Just give Him a day and see what happens.

How do you do this? Start with the small things.

- When you get ready for work and have that extra 10 minutes before you need to go, rather than reading the paper to learn about the world, you read scripture to learn about the kingdom.
- When that coworker decides to criticize and cut you down, rather than becoming part of the problem and retaliating, you take it and attempt to become part of the solution and work past it.
- When you feel that gentle voice telling you that a someone could use encouragement or help, you go give to them, rather than using that time to enjoy the things you want.
- You keep some cash on you so that when you drive or walk by someone who is in need, you can give to them rather than ignore them and go on with your day.

- When you're home from work and want to relax, you choose to help your spouse or kids rather than taking your own time to do what you want.
- When you have a minute to yourself, rather than going immediately for that music or book, you first stop to speak with the Lord and listen.

Basically, when you hit each decision point in your day, you bring God in on it and ask yourself what would glorify Him. In many cases, you already know what would be the right thing to do, and since you've died to yourself today, you choose what would please your Father. When the day's done, stop and take a look at it, then tell me whether you are more pleased with that day than when you choose your path other days.

Do not get frustrated. You're probably not going to do well at the start. I never seem to. Here's one great thing about that verse. When it asks you to take up your cross daily, you can take that two different ways. First, you must commit each day. If you don't start the day making the choice, you will fail. Secondly, each day is a new chance. Perhaps yesterday you failed, but today is another day. You can start over and reach for Him again. Commit yourself to the Lord, but be honest with Him. There may be areas that you realize you aren't ready to commit completely to Him. If this is the case, then bring it to Him and ask Him to work with you to break free from them. Don't expect to be able to give everything up overnight. Perhaps some people can do well with that, but most of us work through it with His help.

There are points in your life where you must count the cost. You face up to fact that you can't do this on your own, and if you want to continue to grow in Jesus, you have to give up your desires. You begin to count the cost of that, you see the areas you need to give up and the decisions that need to be His. It's not easy, and it's definitely not convenient. I've heard it said that God hasn't had a qualified worker yet. You may look at people around you and think how much more qualified everyone is, but when it comes down to it, our choices are what matter. We'll find that all the knowledge and experience falls away in the face of someone who's committed to follow Christ. If you make use of whatever small amount of grace God's given you, God will move. He yearns to move through us. It's not our sins, our lack of knowledge, or our lack of gifts that stop Him. His grace can provide all we need; it's our lack of will that stops Him more than anything.

So how do we know when we're there? How do we know when we've gotten to the point that we have denied ourselves? We can find the end back at the beginning. When you are ready to die, that is when you live. Can you say that you've given up enough of yourself that you are ok with dying if that were to happen today? I believe this is the litmus test for a bond-servant.

> For to me, to live is Christ and to die is gain. — (Philippians 1:21)

When you're ready to physically lose your life for Christ, then you've really begun to gain it. The Lord is our portion. Others can fight for the things of this world, but we can give them up because our heart is with Him. Let's step back to that verse from Romans.

> Therefore I urge you, brethren, by the mercies of God, to present your bodies a living and holy sacrifice, acceptable to God, which is your spiritual service of worship. — (Romans 12:1)

Make your life an offering to the Lord. It is the best act of worship we can provide to the one who so lovingly formed us and provides for us.

Growing

The Friends

One day I found myself in worship at our church singing one of those songs I've sung a hundred times. The chorus of this song says:

> I am a friend of God.
> I am a friend of God.
> I am a friend of God, He calls me friend.

It's a great thought, helping to remind us how close we are to God and what He thinks of us. Yet, on this day, something made me stop singing. My spirit cried out inside of me "ick!" I know that's not so descriptive, but that is the best word I can come up with. It's similar to that feeling you get when you reach under a chair and hit something soft and mushy, then realize you're afraid to find out what you just touched. At this point I stopped, waited quietly, and searched for that feeling. After thinking about it for a minute, I realized I had the feeling because I believed the words of that song weren't true. Oh, it's true for some people, but I don't suppose it is for that many. Looking in the Bible, I have only found 13 people called a friend of God: Abraham, Moses, and the disciples.

> And the scripture was fulfilled that says, "Abraham believed God, and it was credited to him as righteousness," and he was called God's friend. — (James 2:23)

> The LORD would speak to Moses face to face, as one speaks to a friend. — (Exodus 33:11)

> I no longer call you servants, because a servant does not know his master's business. Instead, I have called you friends, for everything that I learned from my Father I have made known to you. — (John 15:15)

Each of these people had a special relationship with God. First, we find Abraham, whose obedience led him out of his land towards God's promises. Next is Moses who talked to God as someone talks to his friend, face to face. Can you say this for yourself? The most interesting group is the disciples. Very clearly, Jesus makes the point that up until then—day before crucifixion—they were servants, but now they will become friends. What does this verse tell us? That we aren't necessarily friends of God. Throughout the Bible we find seasons, situations, relationships and covenants that determine our situations. For this situation we need to look at the context. One of the deceptions from the devil we need to watch for is taking the Bible out of context. We see the disciples called friends, so we assume we must be friends too. Keep in mind, God could use that scripture to speak to you personally and say that you are His friend as well, but that would be the Lord talking to you. When you're reading the Bible, you need to be careful on generalizations of the scripture. If this thought is bothering you, feel free to go to Matthew 4 and read where the Devil quoted several scriptures to Jesus in the wilderness. Scripture used without wisdom and understanding can still deceive. One specific example I have mentioned before was Psalm 91.

> He who dwells in the shelter of the Most High
> Will abide in the shadow of the Almighty.
> I will say to the LORD, "My refuge and my fortress,
> My God, in whom I trust!"
> ...
> You will not be afraid of the terror by night,
> Or of the arrow that flies by day;
> Of the pestilence that stalks in darkness,
> Or of the destruction that lays waste at noon.

> A thousand may fall at your side
> And ten thousand at your right hand,
> But it shall not approach you.
> You will only look on with your eyes
> And see the recompense of the wicked. — (Psalm 91:1–2,5–8)

This passage is often given to people when they come upon hard times. It's a great passage telling of the Lord and what He does for us. Lines like "a thousand may fall at your side, and ten thousand at your right hand, but it shall not approach you" helps give us courage. I have seen these verses on jewelry, pictures, and even made into books. I love this passage and the sense of protection that comes from it. However (I'm sure you knew this was coming), please do not jump past the first verse in your rush to accept the rest for yourself. I'm switching to King James to get a little clearer wording here.

> He who dwells in the secret place of the Most High
> Shall abide under the shadow of the Almighty. — (Psalm 91:1)

Who does David say we will find under the shadow? The one who dwells in the secret place. You can't have the shelter without the time in the secret place. The point I'm making is that being a Christian doesn't mean you have the right to take these verses and claim God will protect you. I believe that most of us understand this intellectually, and yet, I still see us doing it. We tell each other it will be ok, because God will protect us. I am sorry to say it, but that's not the case. God said He will watch over those who dwell in the secret place. If you read a few more verses down, you can find more clarification.

> Because you have made the LORD, who is my refuge,
> Even the Most High, your dwelling place. — (Psalm 91:9)

When you dwell in God, then He will protect you. I'm not going farther on that topic, I only wanted to point out that there is a condition. These promises are for a select group of people.

Levels Of Relationship

I am using Psalm 91 as an example to make my next point clearer. What I have found in the scriptures is that there are different levels of our relationship with God. This is not a "one size fits all" world. Even from the beginning of the law, as we step into Leviticus 1, we find that the burnt offering brought unto the Lord had three different levels as I mentioned earlier. There was the turtledove, the lamb, then the bull. These reveal how much the people were willing to sacrifice to show God their commitment.

Now, bring this into the New Covenant. When a new believer comes to the Lord and asks for forgiveness, asking Jesus to be their Lord, that's a commitment. The problem is, most of us don't fully understand what that means so early in our walk. So typically, salvation is like the turtledove. It costs us, but not a whole lot. Look around, you can trust God for salvation and follow Him, but not pay that much of a cost. The Lord is gracious and understands. This commitment is fine up to a point, but someday God will call you to more. He'll ask for a higher level of commitment. If you want to move on with God, now you need to offer up the lamb. At this level you can't just walk along saying you're a Christian. Perhaps you need to go into the ministry, move to another location, or take up a specific position in God's service. At this level it really starts to hit your everyday life. Continue here faithfully for a while and then God calls you deeper. Now He wants the bull. He wants to take every part of your life, to set aside the things you like to do and choose the things that glorify Him. It hurts, to put aside all those things, in order to make God the one and only part.

If we look back to the temple in the Old Testament, you again find three sections. First you walk into the inner court, then the holy place, and finally the holy of holies. Each area was smaller than the last, and less people were allowed. To enter each one, you follow very strict protocols. We're even told by tradition that the high priest would wear a bell and a rope tied to him in case he went into the holy of holies uncleanly. The requirements were so high that some did not come out on their own. The bell was to alert those outside that they were still alive. The rope, you can guess.

Not only have I found levels of relationship, there are levels of God's will.

> Do not conform to the pattern of this world, but be transformed by the renewing of your mind. Then you will be able to test and approve what God's will is-- his good, pleasing and perfect will. — (Romans 12:2)

Did it ever cross your mind in this scripture that there may be three levels of God's will? I didn't notice it for a long time, thinking them to be merely adjectives for the same will. There's the good will of God. We know God and generally want to please Him but don't know how. His pleasing will takes us a step farther. Maybe we have the leading of the Lord and work toward that, but without good direction. For example, if I felt led to work with kids, I might volunteer in the nursery. Then there's the perfect will. I imagine this is for those who have taken the time to find just exactly what the Lord wants. Like Moses, they know not only that a temple needs to be built, but they have waited to receive the exact dimensions and what it'll take. Personally, I believe this shows a level of commitment to following God that most of us don't desire enough to reach. We stop at getting direction and move on there, not realizing that the Lord wants to reveal and direct even more.

Christians

The main point I want you to understand is that we do not all have the same depth of relationship with God. This is a tough thing to describe as people want to jump on either side of the fence and treat God as either a "demanding boss" or a "you can never do wrong" parent. Some don't have room for something in between. God is so full of grace and love, that getting to heaven is easy and simple, but there is more; so much more. We focus only upon heaven and wonder why we don't reach the world. Look at Paul and his gospel. There you find the crucified life. Let's start with our condition at salvation.

> But as many as received Him, to them He gave the right to become children of God, even to those who believe in His name. — (John 1:12)

I try not to jump into the Greek too often, but I also try not to get talked into playing Barbie with my daughter and yet I still end up playing with Barbies. The word used here for "children" in this verse is "tekna" in Greek. It pretty much means what we read here, a child. There is another word used for the children of God that we may often treat the same, but it is not.

> For all who are being led by the Spirit of God, these are **sons** of God. — (Romans 8:14)

> For the anxious longing of the creation waits eagerly for the revealing of the **sons** of God. — (Romans 8:19)

Here we find the word used for "sons" is a derivative of the word "huios", which means a son who is in the same nature as the father. It's sometimes used in combination with adoption, but from my understanding is meant to be used for a son who has come of age and now has legal rights. This is the word used of Jesus when He was baptized by John the Baptist and God said, "*This is my Son*"(Matthew 3:17). What we find is a distinction between these two. At salvation we are all children of God, having certain rights and privileges that go along with that. However, as we mature to a certain level, we become the mature sons of God and gain authority. We don't yet know what all that means, as creation itself is awaiting the full revelation of those sons, yet it is clearly a deeper walk with God.

Although I have no clear scripture for this, I believe there is a sort of progression to our relationship with God as we mature. First, we are believers, for we accept God, but haven't gone too deep. We mature into disciples who are willing to follow God. As we give more of our lives over, we can move over to bond-servants. This is the title many of the apostles took. Past this, I believe there are several other categories such as the sons of God, the friends of God, and even the bride.

Wait… aren't we all the bride?

That last one still surprises me. I had long been taught that the whole church was the bride of Christ. I believed that until the Lord opened up this verse for me.

> And the angel said to me, "Write this: Blessed are those who are invited to the marriage supper of the Lamb. — (Revelation 19:9)

It took me a bit to catch on and I can distinctly remember when the revelation hit me. I don't remember what started me on this topic, but one day I found myself desiring to know about the marriage of the Lamb. I knew the scripture was in Revelation and searched it down pretty quickly. As I'm pondering that scripture, the middle part caught me. Blessed are those who are invited. Think about it.

Do you invite the bride to the wedding?

Of course not. The wedding is for the bride, you invite the guests to be witnesses and to share in the celebration. What we find here is that the guests of the wedding are blessed, for they were allowed to attend the wedding. That one little statement breaks us up into at least three groups. First, we have the bride of course, then those who are invited to the wedding, and then the rest that aren't.

A couple years ago I had a dream about heaven. I'm going to give the short version here. Basically, I dreamed that I had come to heaven with a group of people that had died. We were brought into heaven with a guide and begin to make our way through. As we walked through different parts of heaven, some of the people were split off to go to their assigned areas in heaven. The overriding thought I can remember having as we went through different areas of heaven, which was a remarkably happy and peaceful place, was that I wanted to be as close to Jesus as possible. Each time a group split off, I was relieved it hadn't been me yet, as I continued to move toward the center of heaven. All I hoped for was to keep moving closer and closer to where the Lord was.

This realization that I may not be part of the bride has hit me hard. I love God. I do. Yet, I obviously love myself as well, and that must be fixed. The God of the universe is willing to call me "His beloved", but can I say the same? You see, many are called, but few are chosen. Not long ago I was spending some time just meditating upon these truths about the bride of Christ, and the Lord spoke to me. Not audible, but this was about as clear a voice in my head as I've ever gotten. He said, "If you want to be my bride, then woo me." Sorry for the slightly archaic wording, but that's what He said and I think it gets the point across. Feel free to substitute court, pursue, charm, attract, or another word that might seem more fitting for you. The point is, if you want to be the bride, make Jesus fall in love with you. That changes everything in the relationship. No longer do I do the right thing so I get to heaven, or don't receive judgements for my shortcomings. Nor am I trying to gain points to get specific rewards. I'm being judged to see if I'm worthy of my beloved.

You didn't think the eternal judgements of God were just about sin did you? You are judged for the good and the bad. Rewards to those who have done well, punishments to those who have not. In heaven we will be judged and receive our rewards. There are crowns for those who have overcome. Positions and levels for those who have earned them. And relationship for those who get through it all and please Him for love's sake.

But I'm Not Like Them

> But from those who were of high reputation (what they were makes no difference to me; God shows no partiality)--well, those who were of reputation contributed nothing to me. — (Galatians 2:6)

Do not raise up some people as more special to God because of their position or title. I have seen this, and done it myself, as well. We think of the "godliest" people as those who are preachers, ministers, missionaries, or staff. I wonder if we think that if we're not up front in the church, we can't be as close to God. We still think well of others, but in a different way. When we think about being closer with God, there is a tendency to think of service, not friendship. We are all part of the same body, and the fact that some are called as ministers does not make them closer to God. If you want to be closer to God, be more like Jesus.

> Be holy, for I am holy — (1 Peter 1:16)

There are no "special" parts, but members of the same body. What can confuse us are the gifts required. A person called as a prophet or apostle require certain gifts to operate. Those with more gifts might seem to be more godly, yet the gifts may only show what was required as part of their calling. God equips His servants for what they need. Just because someone has more than another, this does not make them a better Christian. We must major on the relationship and the fruit, not the gifts.

Beginnings

> For who has despised the day of small things? — (Zecharaih 4:10)

How does this work? We start small, then grow. Think of the

mustard seed, which is a small seed but grows into a large plant. Or remember the parable of the talents. The servant was faithful with one talent, so the master doubled his portion. If we're not faithful with what we've been given, we shouldn't expect more. It's not a matter of righteousness, as in a lack of sin, for that was dealt with. Rather, it's a matter of trust and obedience. If God gives you a small word of direction and you don't listen to it, why should He speak something greater to you. You must be faithful with the small things He's given, then you are able to receive more of Him.

> He who is faithful in a very little thing is faithful also in much; and he who is unrighteous in a very little thing is unrighteous also in much. — (Luke 16:10)

God showed this to me the other day through a situation that came my way. One of my relatives died. After it happened, I found myself stuck on the big questions like why did they die, could I have done anything about that, and how could I help the whole family with this. Yet in all my thinking, I missed that my wife needed my touch. I missed the compassion of confiding in her and talking with her while I was dwelling on the big things that I couldn't change anyway. In thinking about the bigger things, I missed the smaller ones, and missed my chance to make a difference. Do not be frustrated because you feel like you need to completely turn your life around. Be content that you're changing the small things, and God will lead you on to the bigger ones when you're ready. Also, don't spend all your time trying to learn everything.

> But beyond this, my son, be warned: the writing of many books is endless, and excessive devotion to books is wearying to the body. — (Ecclesiastes 12:12)

Strange scripture to hear from someone writing a book; however, I don't write just to write. I'm not writing this to make money, to start a career, or to be famous. I'm writing because the Lord led me to do so. I've learned in my own way, when I devote excessive time to books or sermons, that I burn out. Sure, I'm encouraged for a bit, but I find myself setting aside "knowing God" in order to learn about Him. What's the point of knowledge if it's not used? In the past I have focused so much on knowledge, that I never got around to making use of the knowledge I had. Live the life you can. Then learn more to live more. Growing takes time. You can't rush relationship. Love God and it will fall into place. The devil will use your "works" against you. He will get you so busy doing works for God, studying the Bible, and listening to preachers or Christian music, that you don't grow in your relationship with God. He will try to get you to esteem the "works" of God more than God himself. If you don't spend time with Him, you cannot grow.

Growing

> For this very reason, make every effort to add to your faith goodness; and to goodness, knowledge; and to knowledge, self-control; and to self-control, perseverance; and to perseverance, godliness; and to godliness, brotherly kindness; and to brotherly kindness, love. For if you possess these qualities in increasing measure, they will keep you from being ineffective and unproductive in your knowledge of our Lord Jesus Christ. But if anyone does not have them, he is nearsighted and blind, and has forgotten that he has been cleansed from his past sins. Therefore, my brothers, be all the more eager to make your calling and election sure. For if you do these things, you will never fall, and you will receive a rich welcome into the eternal kingdom of our Lord and Savior Jesus Christ.
> — (2 Peter 1:5–11)

This passage is one of my favorites. I realized it's importance in my life as I read the last section where it tells us that these qualities will keeping us from being ineffective and unproductive. I don't know about you, but one of my biggest fears is to come before the Lord and find that I didn't measure up. Not that I was unsaved, but that I find He is not proud of me. Just like my earthly father, I want to make my heavenly Father proud. I want Him to look upon me and say "good job." As such, I'm sometimes concerned that I have let myself be misguided from His ways. For this reason, when I read these verses, I want to hold on and pursue it to ensure that I am effective and productive for Him. What I appreciate about this passage is that it gives us a path. If we will look at ourselves, and push ourselves to continue to work into these things, they will keep us from failing. That means if you can read through these verses and you do not find yourself striving for one of these steps, you should look at where you are and what you're up to, for fear that you've fallen off track.

"Make every effort"
Another version says, "with all diligence." This isn't like taking a scripture as a good saying, slapping it onto a bracelet, and doing it when we remember. No, being diligent is to be all over it, to have your constant attention on it. We take the truth and meditate upon it, letting it dwell in our minds as we go through our day. Our life should revolve around it, and not merely do it when we have free time.

"Add to your faith"
Faith tells us that we are a child of God and that God has saved us. Faith is the beginning of our journey; a constant friend that guides us along the way. Faith is an essential element to mix in with all the other ingredients. It's like the egg in baking a cake; without it nothing will stick together. Faith comes before anything else, for we must believe before we can understand.

"Goodness"
The next step is goodness, for as our faith shows us that God loves us, we want to return that back to Him. We grow in our desire to obey Him, bless Him, and share Him with others. In this way,

we want to return His goodness back to Him and others around us. Another translation uses the phrase, "moral excellence". This isn't a good effort at doing the right things to those around us, but a drive to excellence in our overall morality. In all things we strive to do our best to bless others because our faith has shown how God has blessed us. Many of us can get stuck here because we are willing to do what looks good to others, but not what looks good to God.

<u>"And to goodness, knowledge"</u>

As we strive to share God's goodness with the world, we must begin to seek out knowledge of how we can help others and please God. I can think of two parts to this. One is knowing how we can please God—the good things to do—and the other is removing the bad things in us as well. I must know them to move past them. To grow deeper, we must know how.

> Search me, O God, and know my heart; try me and know my anxious thoughts; and see if there be any hurtful way in me, and lead me in the everlasting way. — (Psalm 139:23–24)

<u>"And to knowledge, self-control"</u>

As we learn the things that are good(and bad), that is where self-control comes in; because we often know what should be done, but we don't always do it. Self-control takes the knowledge we've found, and changes our lives to incorporate it.

<u>"And to self-control, perseverance"</u>

Then comes perseverance. We know what to do, we have the self-control to do it once, but can we keep doing it over and over. I for one get stuck here a lot. I know what to do, sometimes I do it, but I don't always persevere in it. I may make it a couple days, or a couple weeks, but eventually I get tired. Perseverance is to take that self-control, and hold firm to it no matter what. As James 1:4 says, "perseverance must finish its work."

"And to perseverance, godliness"

This one is my favorite. As we practice perseverance, it leads to godliness. This is when the act of persevering in God's love breaks through. Even though we struggle in our perseverance, we overcome that area and begin to shine out for others. Godliness is not when we're free from temptation, but when we can walk with control during tribulation. Godliness says that in the midst of our struggles, in the midst of our pain, in the midst of our problems, it's still all about our Lord.

When I was in the middle of a certain big struggle in my life, I remember coming to Lord and crying out for help. I had been persevering far past what I had done in the past. I was coming to the end of myself, but the temptations didn't seem to be lessening. I felt like even though I kept resisting, it wasn't getting easier. I knew there was something I needed. I could feel a step that must be taken to move past my perseverance into the Lord's godliness. I felt as if God was leading me to this, so I asked for a verse to help me express what I was feeling. What came into my thoughts was Colossians 3:23. Here's the best part, I didn't even recognize that scripture. Typically, I get a verse I remember, and not a Bible reference. I wasn't even sure if it sounded familiar until I read it later that day.

> Whatever you do, work at it with all your heart, as working for the Lord, not for men. — (Colossians 3:23)

We don't persevere for ourselves. We don't persevere for our family or friends. We persevere because it's our worship unto the Lord. We "offer our bodies as living sacrifices"(Romans 12:1) unto the Lord. God spoke to me once and said, there's no easy path to purity. Now don't get me confused here as I'm not talking pure from forgiveness. I mean purity of our lives. Our sins may be forgiven, but to become godly means living in purity over time so it can be proved. This kind of living can only come through perseverance of trials over time. As we persevere, we start showing His love no matter what.

"And to godliness, brotherly kindness"

The last two steps are acts of will—and of God's grace—but they lead more to a state of change in us. As we fight to do what is right, we change. Our heart becomes more like His. In godliness, we begin to look less at ourselves and more at others, leading us to brotherly kindness. In the midst of whatever you have going on, you can reach out of your circumstances to help a brother, because you've learned to look past yourself. This is much more than just taking care of a brother, this is putting family ahead of yourself. This is the point where you find yourself beginning to think of their happiness before you even think of yours.

"And to brotherly kindness, love"

Finally love. It all leads to love. Love is both the beginning and the end goal. Love is not a feeling, but a person. To reach this love, is to begin to know the mystery that has been revealed in this age, "Christ in us, the hope of glory" (Colossians 1:27).

> For in Christ Jesus neither circumcision nor uncircumcision has any value. The only thing that counts is faith expressing itself through love.
> — (Galatians 5:6)

Keep Contending

If we stop straining, we stop growing. Beware of complacency in your walk where you become comfortable with what you have. Always look for more of God.

Why should we strive so hard to grow? There are a lot of reasons, but I'm only going to give you one. We grow to become mature sons (and daughters) of God. Because only the mature can receive their inheritance.

PART 3 - THE PATH

For the gate is small and the way is narrow that leads to life, and there are few who find it.

— (Matthew 7:14)

The Beginning of Wisdom

> My son, if you will receive my words and treasure my commandments within you, make your ear attentive to wisdom, incline your heart to understanding; for if you cry for discernment, lift your voice for understanding; if you seek her as silver, and search for her as hidden treasure; then you will discern the fear of the Lord and discover the knowledge of God.
> — (Proverbs 2:1–5)

God has much prepared for us. The kingdom has come and the riches of God are available for us. He is ready to bestow His inheritance upon those who have made themselves ready. All this is just waiting to be found if we have the wisdom not only to find this truth, but to make use of it. I'm not going to go over scriptures that speak of wisdom and foolishness. You can feel free to read through Proverbs, but I'll do a quick paraphrase and just say "seek wisdom." Wisdom leads us in the right direction, keeping us from error. Wisdom saves us from many troubles and quickly directs us to our greatest life. Where then do we begin? As it is said, "the journey of a thousand miles begins with a single step." Sometimes that first step is the hardest part. Our path to wisdom and fullness of God begins in the verse above, but is made much clearer in the next.

> The fear of the Lord is the beginning of wisdom —
> (Proverbs 9:10)

The fear of the Lord. Before I take a shot at this topic, I want to discuss one of the core issues which I believe causes us a major problem in our walk today. Do we really believe? We may go to church, give thanks for our meals, and live like good people; however, do we really believe in God? Do we believe that He is out there, that He created everything, that He is in control of it all, and that the Word He has given us is His voice? For most of us, I do not think we believe this with all our hearts. If we did, we would be different. I suspect you have seen the result of someone who does believe. The world probably looks at them like they have a screw loose, but you've seen the truth in their eyes and the belief behind their actions. If we really believed, our lives would show it.

Over and over I have been impressed by how much we know about God, and how little we act upon that knowledge. I guess impressed maybe isn't the right word, I suppose disheartened is more appropriate. With all our Bible translations, devotionals, Bible studies, Sunday schools, blogs, small groups, and internet archives, we are overwhelmed with information about God. Regardless of this, even the truth of the simple fact that Jesus died for us should impact every aspect of our lives. In everything we do, in everything we say, just knowing that God is near should provoke such a transformation in our lives! Too often it's like we don't notice or that it's not that big of a deal. I recognize this behavior because I do this myself. How can I live my life the same way when the God who created me is out there watching?

I would like you to make a choice now. Do you really believe in the Bible? Do you believe in Jesus? If you don't, then I can't help you. You might as well stop reading this book here, because if you aren't set on this, then you can explain away anything else I will say. But for those of you who have chosen to believe, we have a chance.

> But in every nation the man who fears Him and does what is right is welcome to Him. — (Acts 10:35)

Fearing the Lord is where our journey begins. If we want a change, we look to wisdom and find the beginning of wisdom is to fear the Lord. This is a phrase that's often used both in the Old Testament and the New Testament. We read it in scriptures, but seem to gloss over it. It's like we all have the basic understanding of fearing

God, but we rarely stop to talk about it. I've had some discussions recently in which the fear of God popped up, and it was hard for any of us to describe what this fear is. I can tell you this; it's not a normal fear like being afraid of the dark, though there is a portion of that in it. Some might say that being under the new covenant, we don't need fear anymore. They might believe that it was for those in the Old Testament who dealt with a God of punishment and wrath. If you believe this way, that fear isn't a part of our lives, then let me say something that might surprise you. Jesus feared the Lord.

> Then a shoot will spring from the stem of Jesse, and a branch from his roots will bear fruit. The spirit of the Lord will rest on Him, the spirit of wisdom and understanding, the spirit of counsel and strength, the spirit of knowledge and the fear of the Lord. And He will delight in the fear of the Lord, and he will not judge by what His eyes see, nor make a decision by what His ears hear; but with righteousness He will judge the poor, and decide with fairness for the afflicted of the earth. — (Isaiah 11:1–4)

As I said, Jesus feared God. It might seem strange as Jesus is God, yet there it is. That tells us that fear isn't about judgement for sins. On top of that, the fear of the Lord is one of the seven Spirits of God mentioned in this passage. This "fear" is a core ingredient of the working of the Holy Spirit.

Do We Fear God?

> Transgression speaks to the ungodly within his heart; there is no fear of God before his eyes. For it flatters him in his own eyes concerning the discovery of his iniquity and the hatred of it. The words of his mouth are wickedness and deceit; he has ceased to be wise and to do good. He plans wickedness upon his bed;

he sets himself on a path that is not good; he does not despise evil. — (Psalm 36:1–4)

Here we see several traits concerning those who have no fear of God. They go on in sin without caring. They lie, they corrupt, and they plot evil. Even more, they are too prideful of themselves to realize their own problems. I think this makes sense to most of us. This type of person has no fear or respect of God, so why should they even try to be good. They do their own thing, and find enjoyment in that. We have all seen people like this. These verses give us a view of the extreme, so before we go thinking that's no us, let's look for the tendencies within ourselves.

- Do you pray to God in pretty words and religious phrases, or in a humble heart?
- When you speak of God to others, is it to lift up your knowledge and understanding, or to lift them up?
- When you sing before the church, is it to show your voice or His glory?
- When you speak of another, do you show fault to make yourself better or lift up and encourage?
- When you find yourself in conflict with family, do you argue because you are right, or do you broker peace?
- When you see the poor, do you look down upon them for their life choices or do you look with compassion on their brokenness?
- Do you worry and fret over your life, or do you rest easily in peace with the Lord?

You see, there are few of us who fear God enough to walk well. We condone it by looking at others who are worse than us, rather than comparing ourselves to a holy God.

God Is In Control

The first aspect of fear is the respect for power. There is a natural tendency to fear something that has the ability to bring us harm. For example, imagine yourself walking up behind a horse and hitting it. You know better than to do this as the horse could kick you and injure you severely. Similarly, we don't jump in front of a moving car either. Fear can also be a healthy respect, similar to the respect we give people in authority over us such as our parents, bosses, and governments. Let's use the police as an example. Whenever I'm driving down the road and see a police car, suddenly everything changes. I become alert, watch my speed, and pay closer attention to how I'm driving. I make sure I am doing everything correctly. Why is that? I know the officer has authority over me and can give me a ticket, so I watch myself. Even this is such a small scale of what we should feel. If we lived in a true monarchy, that would probably be a better example. Imagine having a king over us that could choose our fate at a whim. In the western world, we seem to have lost much of the fear and respect for our leaders. Even so, having authority nearby helps keep us from making the wrong choices because of our respect for them. Yet, we flaunt our sins in front of a God who sees them all. We know He is there, yet we have so little fear, respect, and love for Him, that we don't mind doing things for Him to see. Does there seem to be something wrong with this behavior?

> Do not fear those who kill the body but are unable to kill the soul; but rather fear Him who is able to destroy both soul and body in hell. — (Matthew 10:28)

God is the ultimate authority over our lives. In His hands are not only our future but our very existence.

> Thus says the LORD, "Heaven is My throne and the earth is My footstool Where then is a house you

could build for Me? And where is a place that I may rest?" "For My hand made all these things, Thus all these things came into being," declares the LORD. — (Isaiah 66:1–2a)

I think those words lay it out. God wanted to make it clear where our place is, and guess what? We are not God. Could we even strive to build something for Him when the earth is His footstool? Why would He even take notice of us? Sometimes I begin my prayers with "You are God, and I am not", just to remind myself of this fact. Think about how big the universe is. It's so hard to even comprehend that most of us never try. The universe is so big that we cannot even see it all yet. Our world is part of one galaxy, the Milky Way. Astronomers believe it has about 100 billion stars in it. That's right, 100,000,000,000 stars. Now, astronomers estimate there are 100 billion galaxies in our universe. Among these 10,000,000,000,000,000,000,000 stars that we believe exist, we live near one of these stars on this one little planet we call earth. How big does that make our God who can create such a wonder?

Tell me then, how is it we can be so cavalier with God? How is it we can walk in front of the God who created all this and not be affected by Him every moment of the day? I would like to say it's because we don't realize it's Him, but in many cases, we don't have that excuse. We have the Word of God written in a book. We read it often and hear it spoken to us, but it doesn't really move us? Shouldn't a word from the almighty God shake us to the core? The passage I quoted above from Isaiah continues:

> But to this one I will look, to him who is humble and contrite of spirit, and who trembles at My word. — (Isaiah 66:2)

The first thing I want to point out is that God sees us. We might be but mere specks in this universe, and yet God Almighty takes notice of us. Next, He even pays attention to certain people. That's just crazy. Lastly, He looks to those who tremble at His word. It's only recently that I began to get some understanding there. Let me tell you a quick story.

This happened to me when the Lord was really impressing me with this passage for the first time. What I often do, mainly with smaller passages, is memorize the passage so that I can meditate upon it easier. In this case I was interested in these verses for the second part of verse 2, the part that tells us that God looks to him who is humble, contrite in spirit, and trembles at His word. Like I mentioned above, God takes notice of those, so I was wanting to understand that better. Little did I know that God was going to help clear this up. There's really nothing like learning the Word through experience. One day I'm walking in to work and I found myself complaining to the Lord. You see, I had been listening to messages from ministers I consider to be men and women of faith. I listened to the stories about things God's done in their lives and around them. There was one particular story about a man who received visions from God to teach him truths from the scriptures. That has not been how I have learned, so here I was complaining to God about why some people seem to get more help than others. Why is it that some people have these dreams and visions and others do not? Why does God seem to give certain people more to validate His word and presence than others? Of course, what I'm really saying is, "why don't I get this?" As I'm talking, there's a small part of me that realizes that it is not my place to make this type of criticism; which is what I was doing. I don't think it's wrong to want more or even to question God as to why, but that wasn't what I was doing. I was criticizing God. Then, in the middle of my complaints that voice comes into my head. I hope you know that voice, and if not you will come to recognize it as you spend more time with the Lord. It's that voice that comes and says something into your thoughts that is so immediate and different than what you were thinking, you know it's from elsewhere. Here is what I heard:

"You can hear my voice, what more do you need?"

That stopped me cold. Literally, I'm in the middle of the hallway of my building, walking toward my desk, and I just stopped. I'm lucky there wasn't someone right behind me or they would have run into me. It took me a couple seconds to even get moving again. It's as if my mind got stuck for the rest of the walk. What do you do when God says something like that? Is there any response you can give when the maker of the universe decides to correct you? It wasn't even harsh, but all I know is that I suddenly got scared. I think deep down I realized what I had just done and had a little glimpse of how real God is and it shook me. All it took was a little glimpse and I got worried. If the earth is His footstool, what does that make us? On top of that, what do you think goes through God's mind when we come and tell Him how it should be done. It's a good thing that the Lord has so much patience. I've come to value those times that I tremble. In them, I come to see a little more clearly. I want to be shaken by His Word. His Word created everything we know; its value is beyond what we can imagine. A word from God is more precious than any of our riches.

One other small but very significant reason to keep in mind of why we should fear the Lord is that He knows what will happen. How often do you think God tries to warn us of trouble we're about to get into and we don't listen? This isn't just for the consequences of our sin, because often we are willing to accept the consequences of sin so we can get what we want. Rather, this could be the flight that crashed, the day that bad wreck happened on the interstate, or the thieves that could've run across your path. I have heard many stories of God speaking to someone to not take a trip, slow down, or other sorts of warnings that kept them out of danger.

God Is Not Tame

In "Chronicles of Narnia", there is a lion named Aslan who is one of the central figures of the book. He is a sort of mythical leader of the kingdom of Narnia, who shows up when the nation is in need. In many ways, he represents Jesus in the book. There's a statement made about Aslan in this book that makes an important point about

God that I believe many Christians need to keep in mind. Lucy is one of the main characters in the book and is a young girl who finds her way into Narnia. Lucy hears from Mr. Beaver about Aslan for the first time. Being a young girl, hearing about a lion frightens her. She asks the questions few of us even think to wonder about God, but Lucy being young and innocent just spits it out. She asks Mr. Beaver if Aslan is a tame lion. The Beaver laughs and replies: "Tame, of course he's not tame, but he's good."

We find it comforting to place God into the box we've built for Him. We learn our doctrines, figure out how things fit, and attempt to go about our lives; only to find that our nice little view of the world doesn't pan out. We lose our job and complain it isn't fair. We have a family member die and ask why God would do this to us. We have something taken from us and claim that we deserved it. Over the years, I have come to realize that religion (feel free to replace this with doctrine or theology) is the box we put around God to make Him fit into a world we can live in. I heard a quote once that went like this, "One day I realized God and I were incompatible and one of us had to change." God doesn't stay in the doctrines we've made for Him. He is God. Things happen that we can't explain. As we grow, He wants us to understand His ways, but He does things for His own reasons and not according to what we might consider right. God isn't concerned about whether His decisions seem fair to us. He is righteous, so He will do what is right. Jesus demonstrated this to those around Him many times while He was here. Here are two scriptures I want you to read about Jesus to make my next point.

> "But so that you may know that the Son of Man has authority on earth to forgive sins," – He said to the paralytic – "I say to you, get up, and pick up your stretcher and go home." Immediately he got up before them, and picked up what he had been lying on, and went home glorifying God. They were all struck with astonishment and began glorifying God;

and they were filled with fear, saying, "We have seen remarkable things today." — (Luke 5:24–26)

The angel said to the women, "Do not be afraid; for I know that you are looking for Jesus who has been crucified. He is not here, for He has risen, just as He said. Come, see the place where He was lying. Go quickly and tell His disciples that He has risen from the dead; and behold, He is going ahead of you into Galilee, there you will see Him; behold, I have told you." And they left the tomb quickly with fear and great joy and ran to report it to His disciples. — (Matthew 28:5–8)

Why were the people who witnessed these events afraid? In both instances wonderful things happened, but the people left with fear. Why should they be afraid when God worked a loving miracle before their eyes. The problem was that God moved in a way that they weren't prepared for. It's difficult to have your understanding of the world turned around. It's also difficult to know there's a God calling the shots and you're not the one in control.

It is a terrifying thing to fall into the hands of the living God. — (Hebrews 10:31)

It is frightening to realize that God has His own ideas and may not follow your plans. Even more, God doesn't always do things that seem so wonderful. Remember the priest back with King David who touched the Ark of the Covenant? The priests had clear instructions to never touch the ark, but when they stumbled and started to drop it, one of the priests reached out to steady the ark so it would not fall. God struck him down. You may say, well that was the Old Testament law, God doesn't act like that anymore. If that's so, what about the story of Anias and Saphira? Do you remember their story from Acts? They lied about the amount they sold their land for in front of the church and God; and they died immediately as a result. We must fear the Lord because He can give and He can take away.

Deserving Respect

The last part of fear is to respect someone's character. Not only does God deserve our respect for what He can do, but also for what He has done and who He is. One of the thieves on the cross during Jesus crucifixion understood this part of the fear of the Lord.

> One of the criminals who were hanged there was hurling abuse at Him, saying "Are You not the Christ? Save Yourself and us!" But the other answered, and rebuking him said, "Do you not even fear God, since you are under the same sentence of condemnation? And we indeed are suffering justly, for we are receiving what we deserve for our deeds; but this man has done nothing wrong." And he was saying, "Jesus, remember me when You come in Your kingdom!" — (Luke 23:39–42)

This thief knew enough about who Jesus was to respect Him. Not only did he stand up to the other thief, but he asked Jesus to remember him. This was a thief who did enough to be crucified; yet he gave more respect to our King than some Christians I have met who happily criticize God. In this thief's despair, he put his hope in a God he didn't understand. Rather than rebuking God for his own problems and trying to force Him to act like the other thief had tried, he respected God's decisions and tried to bring himself into what God was doing. I once had a friend tell me, "You can either decide that God isn't there listening, or you can decide that you're done trying to figure out why God does things and just follow Him." That's the fear of the Lord in a nutshell. I don't understand, but He's God, so I'm with Him.

We can learn much of the character of God by looking back

through the scriptures. Look how He has provided time and again for His people. God made sacrifices for us, and He deserves respect for those acts.

> If you address as Father the One who impartially judges according to each one's work, conduct yourselves in fear during the time of your stay on earth; knowing that you were not redeemed with perishable things like silver or gold from your futile way of life inherited from you forefathers, but with precious blood, as of a lamb unblemished and spotless, the blood of Christ. — (1 Peter 1:17-19)

We should conduct ourselves with fear because of the high price that was paid to redeem us. When God first created man, He knew what would happen. He knew the results of giving man the freedom to love Him. Without the choice to love, it's not really love at all. God knew that He would have to sacrifice His own Son for a time. Even so, many of His children would be lost. Can you imagine the pain from knowing that would happen? He knew that He would lose so much if He created us, yet He did it anyway.

Conclusion

> For in many dreams and many words there is emptiness. Rather, fear God. — (Ecclesiastes 5:7)

Fear God. Fear Him with your life and your actions, not just in words. Fear him because He is all-powerful. Fear him because He knows all we do and most especially He knows what is in our hearts. Fear him because he knows what is coming and what is best for us. Fear him because He loves you with a fierce love. Just as a child must learn to fear his parents and obey their word when they don't understand, we must fear God and obey His word, especially when we don't understand why. Of all the people on earth, Jesus alone truly knew God. He understood Him in a way no one else did. He knew of His character, His grace, His love, His power, and His righteousness. He knew better than to turn from His ways, for His ways are good. Jesus feared God for who He is and delighted in it, for God is holy.

The fear of the Lord is the beginning. As we learn his ways, that fear will bring forth love as we see all that He has done before us. God's choice is love. If He wanted fear over all else, He would've come in war; instead, He came as a savior. He came to love.

The Greatest Command

> Hearing that Jesus had silenced the Sadducees, the Pharisees got together. One of them, an expert in the law, tested him with this question: "Teacher, which is the greatest commandment in the Law?" Jesus replied: "'Love the Lord your God with all your heart and with all your soul and with all your mind.' This is the first and greatest commandment." — (Matthew 22:34–38)

Jesus was asked by the leading experts of the time what the greatest command was. They were hoping to catch Jesus in some sort of trap, but Jesus did not respond as they expected. Had I tried to answer this question, I would have gone to the Ten Commandments. God wrote them onto stone, of course the greatest commandment would come from there. Maybe it's the first commandment; that would make sense. Instead, Jesus quoted scripture from Deuteronomy. Love God with everything. This passage has such awesome implications. Of all the laws given throughout the Bible, Jesus singled this out as the greatest. He even went so far as to say of this command and the command to love others that:

> All the Law and the Prophets hang on these two commandments. — (Matthew 22:40)

Talk about a core truth! All that the Law was meant to accomplish was based on these two commands. All the prophets had to say was based on these two commands. This is the greatest command ever given to us, but we fail to give it its rightful place in our lives. We often treat it as a goal rather than a lifestyle. You see, if we put this commandment first, that means every decision we make would keep this in mind. Every action we take would be an outgrowth of this overwhelming love inside us. Every word we speak would come first from our love of Him. Instead, many of us love God in the convenient times. We find ourselves stopping when it gets tough, because we have trouble understanding what He is doing. Other times we stop when things are going well and we feel like we're not in need of the Lord. Then when we get busy, we just plain forget Him because of everything else going on. Look at the words God had for the church of Ephesus.

> I know your deeds and your toil and perseverance, and that you cannot tolerate evil men, and you put to the test those who call themselves apostles, and they are not, and you found them to be false; and you have perseverance and have endured for My name's sake, and have not grown weary. But I have this against you, that you have left your first love. — (Revelation 2:4)

This church sounds like they were doing well. They had worked hard for God, doing His work, and continued in the work through trials. They did not tolerate evil, but uncovered the false leaders sent among them. They stood for truth rather than being politically correct or tolerant. Through all this, they persevered for God's sake under trials. To me this sounds like an amazing church, and yet God said that they had one shortcoming—they had forgotten their first love. So, if a church that is doing this well can lose their love for God, how much more could we? I would dare to say, that where the Ephesian church was in danger of losing their first love, many churches of our age are in danger of never having fully loved at all. We have enough things to occupy us that we don't often have room for God.

Look around and tell me if this is the sort of love you see around you. I see plenty of people that care about each other, but do I see people willing to love enough to confront? How about willing to sacrifice for each other? Are we ready to follow God's lead if it costs us personally? Are we willing to give up our desires for His? In the end, our motives betray us.

> If I give all I possess to the poor, and surrender my body to the flames, but have not love, I gain nothing.
> — (1 Corinthians 13:3)

This verse tells me that if I went to the street corner and emptied my wallet to the man with a sign, then got online and transferred my savings to the Salvation Army, then sold my house and gave the extra to the Red Cross, but did not do it with love; it was all worthless. Our first thought might be, how could this be? How is it that we can give up so much, and yet it does nothing for us? The truth is in the motives. It doesn't matter how it looks or who we give to, it's the motive inside that counts.

> For man looks at the outward appearance, but the LORD looks at the heart. — (1 Samuel 16:7)

In God's eyes, the spirit of our actions is more important than our actions themselves. David went into the temple and took the bread that was for the priests alone, yet God didn't judge him. David was a man after God's own heart and he understood the heart of God well enough to know he could take the bread. Similarly, Jesus picked grains of wheat on the Sabbath, which was forbidden by the Pharisees. Are we more interested in following the letter of the Law, or in loving the God who wrote it?

Why We Don't Love

What then is wrong with us? We have overlooked the greatest of commands among the other concerns of our life. We're so comfortable in our judgmental attitudes, our fleshly natures, and our daily routines that we don't want to put a God first that might stir things up. We are deceived by the devil as to what is most important. In this case, we should think about those things pulling us away. Sin is the obvious first candidate.

> For this is the love of God, that we keep his commandments. — (1 John 5:3)

Our human nature is to sin, we were born with that. Sin has its own reward, though it's short-lived, and it can be hard for us to give that up. This is especially true for those sins that have already ensnared us. We can see the short-term advantage of the sin, and that desire overrides any long-term decisions. When we sin, we show God that the rewards of sin are more important than His commands.

At other times the world pulls us back.

> Do not love the world or anything in the world. If anyone loves the world, the love of the Father is not in him. — (1 John 2:15)

Worldly things can be a distraction. This can be easy, because the world seems more real as we can touch and see it. It's easy to forget what we have in faith when confronted with what we have in the flesh. The things of this world may not be sins, but if they distract us from God, then they have become sin to us. A television can bring us news, weather, and entertainment, but it can also fill us with evil, perversion, and despair. Food itself is not bad, but too much love for it leaves you full in the stomach and empty in the heart.

Lastly our obligations draw us short.

> Martha, Martha, you are worried and bothered about so many things; but only one thing is necessary, for Mary has chosen the good part, which shall not be taken away from her. — (Luke 10:41–42)

We put expectations upon ourselves for what a good and godly person would do. We must be kind to all, give gifts, bring food to the sick, give to the poor, put on a happy face, be there for our families in any problem, listen when we don't have time, and the list goes on. What we forget is that when we attempt to please everyone, we forget to please the One. For instance, having a job is necessary to provide food for the table, but if it leaves us with no time to serve the Lord, then in the end it has distracted us from our true goal. Spending time with our family is an ingredient to a healthy family, yet if that is our whole focus, we leave out Christ as the center. Even the good things, such as church functions, fellowship, and family can pull us away from God. We can get caught up so much in doing what is "right" that we don't do it out of the right spirit. If you become too busy working for God to be with God, you know something is wrong.

If you love Me, you will keep My commandments.
— (John 14:15)

When you choose to be hurtful to someone, you have chosen to indulge your selfish desires over acting as God would desire? When you insult another, you choose to lift yourself up instead of God? When you give into your physical desires, you choose how you feel rather than how God will feel. When you break it down, sin is us choosing something else over God. Yet there is hope, for when you operate in love, everything gets easier.

For example, I've been married for over a decade now. I find that marriage is often a good picture of our relationship with God as we are to be the bride of Christ. So, in our marriage, we would often have those times where one of us gets frustrated and take our anger out on the other. The natural reaction is to dish it back. I, personally, get defensive and point things back at her. My pride gets wounded by what she said, so I feel the need to justify and build myself back up by answering back. I wouldn't yell—I wouldn't even let myself lose control—yet my responses would not resolve the situation. Often in the heat of a dispute, my words just fan the flames of anger. I tried to be better at this. I tried to respond better, but even though I worked on it, it never really got better. That is, until a few years ago.

What changed? My heart. I began to grow deeper in my relationship with the Lord, and I found strength in that relationship. I found more patience, self-confidence and perspective. I now realize (at times) that when my wife or I say something harsh, that this is usually the frustration talking. If I can just keep calm and respond in a gentler way while trying to be understanding with her, we can often find ourselves laughing at the situation within a few minutes(hint: don't laugh at the time, bad idea). When I respond out of my love for her and not my self-righteousness, it can rub off on her and we more quickly move on. As I draw closer with God, my responses to these events change. My heart itself had changed, and I found this sin was easier to control. Conversely, as I get too caught up in the world and not God, my responses suffer as well.

Tell Me Of Love

One of my favorite examples of love for God comes from the story of Joseph in Genesis 39. In this chapter Potiphar's wife was trying to tempt Joseph into sleeping with her. She had been making attempts to seduce him multiple times, and although he tried, he could not avoid her indefinitely. There came a day when she cornered him with no one around and made her advance on him. Listen to Joseph's reply to her offer.

> "With me in charge," he told her, "my master does not concern himself with anything in the house; everything he owns he has entrusted to my care. No one is greater in this house than I am. My master has withheld nothing from me except you, because you are his wife. How then could I do such a wicked thing and sin against God"? — (Genesis 39:8–9)

Joseph was explaining how Potiphar put everything under him except for Potiphar's wife. Yet after this statement, Joseph responds by saying he could never do this to God rather than saying he couldn't do this to Potiphar. Joseph was more worried about hurting God than he was about hurting the position he had with Potiphar. He loved God in such a way that he couldn't imagine doing this sin against Him. If we loved God as we should, we would find sin hard to imagine because we know what God thinks and we wouldn't want to hurt him. If we loved God more than ourselves, we would be willing to persevere to please Him rather than indulging ourselves.

We are unfortunately plagued with doubts. We do not understand God and don't want to trust in someone we aren't sure is for us. We know what the Bible says, but we don't live it out. Instead, how do we respond when God doesn't do what we expect? What if His choice isn't what we feel we need? Can we love God through our own loss? Think of Shadrach, Meshach, and Abednego. When the king ordered them to bow and they didn't, he condemned them to death in the fire. Here is how they answered the king.

> O Nebuchadnezzar, we do not need to give you an answer concerning this matter. If it be so, our God whom we serve is able to deliver us from the furnace of blazing fire; and He will deliver us out of your hand, O king. But even if He does not, let it be known to you, O king, that we are not going to serve your gods. — (Daniel 3:16–17)

Even though they didn't know that God would save them, they still would not bow to another. Their love for their Lord was such that they would give their lives rather than turn against Him. It would be easy to justify the act by telling yourself you still have your life to continue serving God. It was just a gesture right? Except these three didn't see it this way. What an example of love and faithfulness, that they would not do such a simple act and bow to another. Is your love such that you can know that God is able, but that He still may not come to rescue you when you stick up for Him? If you were confronted like Peter at Jesus's trial, would you stand up for what you are, or hide? If you had a life-threatening disease, would your prayer be, "God I know you can heal, but even if you don't, I will serve you"? Does your love for God run so deep you can choose Him over yourself?

Why Love?

If we want to love God more, first we must ask why it is we love Him to begin with. Too often we get caught up with the how of things and not enough of the why.

> Man looks at the outward appearance, but the Lord looks at the heart. — (1 Samuel 16:7)

It matters less what you do than why you do it. In our worldly lives, that's typically not the case, especially in the workplace. However, from a spiritual point of view, if our reasons aren't pure, He knows. It's not like you can pull a fast one over on God. Maybe if you say you love Him so convincingly with such nice words, maybe He won't notice that your heart is not in it. Of course not. We need to truly love Him. So why is it that we should love God? Simple answer:

> We love because He first loved us. — (1 John 4:19)

Don't let the shortness and simplicity of this verse keep you from thinking about it. Before we even had a chance, God loved us. Before we existed, He planned for us. Before we were born, He formed each of us. Before we asked for His grace, He measured it out for us. Before we knew of love, He showed us what it was.

> We know love by this, that He laid down His life for us. — (I John 3:16)

It's time to play the "what I didn't notice for the first 20 years as a Christian" game. If you read the verse too quickly you will read something like, "we know He loved us because He died for us." Even saying that, you may not have caught the little difference there. It didn't say we know *His love* by this, but that we know *love* by this. You need to forget your definition of love. We know our world has a crazy view of love. If you read enough books and watch enough movies, you will come to believe that love is something you fall into and out of. Love is something you have for that friend who takes care of you or for those poor people who need food and clothing. You'll find that it's something you can find from looking at someone's appearance or how they act. God knows better, as He is love. Love is more a choice than a feeling. John was telling us to know love by what Jesus sacrificed for us. Use that to define love, then learn to love the same way.

> For I am convinced that neither death, nor life, nor angels, nor principalities, nor things present, nor things to come, nor powers, nor height, nor depth, nor any other created thing, will be able to separate us from the love of God, which is in Christ Jesus our Lord. — (Romans 8:38-39)

Now that is love. We need to become convinced of God's love toward us. When we are convinced of how much He loves us, we will find ourselves with no choice but to love a God so overwhelmingly in love with us.

> Therefore, I tell you, her many sins have been forgiven--as her great love has shown. But whoever has been forgiven little loves little. — (Luke 7:47)

Love and forgiveness go together. For the one who felt like he was forgiven little, he will love little in return, but for the one who understands he is forgiven much, he will love much. We need to remember two things about this. First, we shouldn't forget about the depths of sin God has saved us from. We often don't think much about how far we pulled away from God and how we've rebelled against Him. In a bit of irony, the good news is that we continue to make bad choices, and as such we continue to see God's grace in action. When we've forgotten from what depths God pulled us from, we've forgotten how much He loved us and how much we owe him. Secondly, remember the price Jesus paid. Have you ever just stopped, closed your eyes, and attempted to imagine what Jesus went through in those last 24 hours? Have you thought about how He felt during the betrayal, with the disciples fleeing, the scourging, the beatings, the crown of thorns, the cross, and the ridicule? Then, worst of all, He felt the separation. He didn't cry out to God to take the pain away. No, He cried out "my God, why have you forsaken me?" That was His deepest pain. Not the pain of the flesh, but the loss of the Father's presence and love.

How To Love God

Let's step through the greatest command found in Matthew 22:37.

- Love the lord your God

It doesn't say obey, fear, or respect; it says love. Is this different than how we treat Him? Do we treat Him as loving or overbearing? Do we do what is "right" out of our fear of punishment? Have we always made our choices like going to church because we want God on our side or because we love to worship Him? Choose to love God, for this is not something that just happens. Choose and choose again.

- With all your heart

What is it I treasure? What is it that I desire in the deep parts of me? Are all my hopes and dreams rooted in God? Make God your dream. Store up your treasures in Him. Put your hopes upon what He has. Make your goal to please Him. Find your satisfaction in His pleasure.

- With all your soul

How do our actions judge us? Do your emotions betray you?

When you walk into church are you excited or bored? Are you excited about the Lord and what He's doing? Make your life about Him. Your emotions shouldn't lead you, but they are often a good indicator of problems. Use them to see what parts of you aren't the Lord's. Use all your willpower and all your strength to do what is right unto Him.

- With all your mind

What is it that I spend my time on and I think about? When things happen, do I reason from a carnal mind or a spiritual mind? Does every bit of my willpower go to holding onto God in the face of trials? When I know what is right, do I fight to do it? Choose Him. There is a battle in your mind for what you will believe on and what you will think about. Make it Him. Don't fill your mind up with junk, but focus upon the good things. Always give thanks to Him. Think through your actions to make sure they give glory to Him. Here are a couple simple truths that have helped me in my journey to love God more.

1. God is a person

As I've said before, treat God like a person and not a figure. Think about how He might feel in situations. Imagine what Jesus suffered through. God doesn't choose everything that happens in the world, because He's given free will to us. He is involved, He can work it for good, but He doesn't make choices for us. Inevitably, we will make choices that He doesn't like. Therefore, when people hurt Him, do we try to help? Likewise, when you're tempted to sin, remember that He is with you. When you choose something over Him, it hurts Him. It's easy to disregard an organization calling to ask for money, but when it's a friend, it gets personal. Treat God like a person and not like a black box that you throw prayers at and sometimes get an answer back. He's not a grocery store where you bring your shopping list and come home with what you need.

2. Get to know Him

Since God is a person, it makes sense that we can come to know

Him. You see, God's not like a computer, where you find the right combination of keystrokes and you get the output you want; He is a being. We were created in His image, so when we look at ourselves, we're seeing an image of what God is like. Take the time to know Him. Treat Him like you would a friend you want to get to know better. Even better, treat Him like someone you're dating. For those of you who are married, do you remember that time where you first started dating your spouse? You couldn't get enough of them. You found yourself just sitting there asking all sorts of crazy questions just so you could know their history, how they think, and what made them the way they are. The same is true of God. Until you fall in love with Him, you won't come to know Him. The more you find out, the more you will love.

3. Do your best

One thing I have come to appreciate about this command to love God is what was asked of us. Jesus didn't say to love God like Him or to love him perfectly, but to love Him with all we have. Take for example the verses from Romans 8 telling us that we should be convinced of His love. What if I'm not? I know it in my head, but it hasn't reached my heart. So, if I'm not fully convinced of this, if I haven't gotten that revelation of His goodness, it's hard to love that much in return. Yet God made provision. Jesus said to love with all you have. There is no perfect line to reach for us. You love with what's been given you. As you love the Lord, He'll reveal more of Himself to you. With the greater relationship He has given you, comes the ability to love Him even more. As more is given us, more will be expected, but we can only give back what we have. It is up to us to give all we can.

Always Come Back To Love

In John 14–15, we find Jesus and His disciples after the Lord's Supper. Jesus knows He is going to be taken this night and crucified, thus it will be the last time with His disciples together. Jesus tells them of what is to happen, then tells them of the Father and the Spirit that will help them. Next Jesus tells them the secret to bearing fruit.

> I am the vine, you are the branches; he who abides in Me and I in him, he bears much fruit, for apart from Me you can do nothing… Just as the Father has loved Me, I have also loved you; abide in My love — (Matthew 15:5,9)

Jesus taught them to abide in Him and in His love. That is where your strength and your sustenance comes from—Jesus's love. Abiding in His love is important for "God is love"(1 John 4:8). Whenever I find myself lost and confused about where I am headed, I like to come back to this. What I have found is that if I am looking for where God is working, then I should be looking for love being poured out. That is where He will be.

> Be on the alert, stand firm in the faith, act like men, be strong. Let all that you do be done in love. — (1 Corinthians 16:13-14)

Prayer

We were made to know God.

Even after writing a whole chapter on this topic, I still stop and wonder at this truth. It's as if this whole book is summed up in that one statement. When we grasp that statement, our world will change.

If we want to know Him, then we must talk with Him, which leads us to prayer. At its heart, prayer is our communication with God. It's a simple idea that I have found to be complicated and difficult to practice productively in my life. I was saved when I was 10 years old, yet at the age of 30 I still found myself stopping and wondering if I knew how to pray. Listening to the words that came out of my mouth, I realized how little life and power were in them. Instead I heard the phrases I had learned from others, repeated in a way that I hoped would get a response. I have found that when we come to the point of realizing that our prayers sound repetitive and our requests sound memorized, we can know that something has gone wrong. In my life, my requests had become too much like a fast-food drive thru instead of a relationship with a person.

The Silly Things We Do

Before we speak about prayer, let's discuss some of our bad habits

<u>Flowery Words</u>

Have you ever heard someone come before the church and pray in the King James? "O Holy God, watch over us, thy people, shelter us under thy wings and hearken unto our supplication." I'd like to say this is an embellishment, but I have heard prayers come close to this. Some people will make their prayers more dramatic by using archaic wording to give them a flourish and make them sound more biblical. Who do you think they are trying to impress? Was it not the Pharisees who loved to pray out in public to be heard by others that were the most condemned by Jesus(Matthew 6:5)? A few stumbled words from a broken heart are worth more to God than a thousand flowery words from a dignified but stoic speaker.

Empty Words

On one occasion I found myself praying for a friend for whom I had received direction from the Lord. I hadn't found the time to act on it yet, so as I worked through my list and came to their request again, I prayed again. As I prayed, I felt in the spirit that my prayer went dry. This was during one of those wonderful prayer times where the Lord seemed to be near, so I immediately stopped and stayed still for a minute, wondering in my heart about it. That's when God said, "empty prayers mean nothing to me." This made me realize that God had given me something to do, and until I had acted upon it I shouldn't be uttering the same request over and over again, as if sheer repetition will change things for my friend. As I thought about it, it reminded me of the Gentiles in Matthew 6:6 who "suppose that they will be heard for their many words." Words become meaningless when they become a pattern.

Ritual does nothing for us

When you pray, do you often find yourself repeating certain requests in your prayers like I do? Phrases like "God be with me today", "bless this food for our bodies", or "make me like Jesus". These are wonderful phrases that probably meant a lot to me when I first used them. I remember one instance where I asked the Lord how His day was, which had become my custom at the beginning of each day. In this particular instance, I unexpectedly heard an immediate response. Rather than God responding to my question I was asking, God said to me, "you know I don't answer to your rituals." Ouch. I hadn't realized that so quickly I had gone from asking Him how He was doing today, to making that one of my steps to try and get into the spirit. Unfortunately, what I fell into was coming to ask about Him only as a step toward something else I desired, and not as an act of love. This brought a greater understanding concerning the time when Jesus told the Pharisees that He desired mercy and not sacrifice (Matthew 9:13). He will take sorrow over ritual any day.

Who's in charge?

Another mistake we make is when we ask God to do the things that we should do ourselves. A good example is when I would pray "God, help me to love you more". On the surface, this sounds like a nice, religious prayer. Now, let's suppose I were to ask my wife, "Honey, can you help me love you more?" How do you think that would work out for me? Would it make her feel like I love her or that I'm trying to drop the burden upon her for my inadequacy? The temptation is to take the whole problem and throw it upon God to ease our conscious. We attempt to make prayer the end and not the beginning. It's sneaky how this laziness can move in on us. James described a similar situation as those who told the poor to "be warmed and well fed", but did nothing for them (James 2:14-17). Beware when you ask prayers for things you can do yourself. Don't drop your duties upon God.

Prayers for comfort

For a couple months, I was in a men's discipleship group with my brother. One day he shared a revelation which has stayed on my heart ever since. He told us that for years he had been praying a specific way, until the day he realized that the majority of his prayers had to do with his comfort. He would pray for health for his family, protection over them, food for the table, help in issues they were dealing with, and blessings upon them. It hit him then how self-centered his prayers had become. I'm reminded of this often when I pray. Am I more concerned about my own comfort, or of the love of God being shown to the world? This just goes to show my lack of faith in God. "But if God so clothes the grass of the field, which is *alive* today and tomorrow is thrown into the furnace, *will He* not much more *clothe* you? You of little faith!" (Matthew 6:30). God is a loving Father, so we should be much more focused upon what we can do for others than upon what God can do for us.

Self-centeredness

Do you have any of those friends who seem to only listen to you long enough to turn the conversation back to them? I have had full conversations with friends where nothing about me is ever said. As a friend, you are interested and listen, but it can be wearing that they don't seem to be interested in you. God can feel the same. Because He is such a good God, He is interested and will listen and respond to us, but He won't involve you in the things He has going on because you don't care to ask. How much do we miss because we are so short-sided?

Whose Name

Have you ever asked yourself why we end our prayers with "and I ask this in Jesus name, Amen"? I have. I question things, it's just one of those things I do. Big shock, huh? There are probably many Christians who have never thought to question, and many others that have but still don't know why. Like I've said before, there's knowledge and then there's revelation. We may have heard the reasons why, but if it's not down in your heart where truth lives, then it's not doing you much good. Here is what I suspect to be the source of this Christian tradition.

> Whatever you ask in My name, that will I do, so that the Father may be glorified in the Son. — (John 14:13)

Many of us have been taught this verse; that if we ask in Jesus name, then God answers our prayers. I suspect we have all also come to the conclusion that just adding those words alone won't make our prayers be answered. Yet, we continue. Oh, we probably realize this has something to do with it being part of His will, but this concept comes a little too close to me pointing, saying "abra cadabra", and pretending something will happen. Why else would this become such a staple response? We seem to believe that adding His name gives our prayers more validity, but that's not how it works. Instead, let's look to Peter and John.

> Now Peter and John were going up to the temple at the ninth hour, the hour of prayer. And a man who had been lame from his mother's womb was being carried along, whom they used to set down every day at the gate of the temple which is called Beautiful, in order to beg alms of those who were entering the temple. When he saw Peter and John about to go into the temple, he began asking to receive alms. But Peter, along with John, fixed his gaze on him and said, "Look at us!" And he began to give them his attention, expecting to receive something from them. But Peter said, "I do not possess silver and gold, but what I do have I give to you: In the name of Jesus Christ the Nazarene—walk!" And seizing him by the right hand, he raised him up; and immediately his feet and his ankles were strengthened. With a leap he stood upright and began to walk; and he entered the temple with them, walking and leaping and praising God. — (Acts 3:1–8)

Did mentioning the name of Jesus make this man walk? Would that prayer have worked if they had just told Him to walk or asked God? I have asked questions like this before, but the conclusion I have come to is that this is the wrong question. I found myself starting by asking why praying in Jesus name would help to get prayers answered. Notice that I was trying to figure out what to change in my life and in my prayers in order to make them more likely to be answered. My focus became getting my prayers answered and not the prayer itself. The real question is, what will please the Lord. Forget yourself. Forget the things you want. Forget what you think is right. God is all. Look at what Jesus did, what He said, what He wanted, and then pray for those things to happen. He is the same yesterday, today, and forever (Hebrews 13:8). Jesus wanted God's name glorified, His sheep cared for, and the truth to be made known. This comes down to the heart of prayer. Prayer is not about getting what we want, but about accomplishing God's work on this earth. Asking in His name is not making our prayers match to some formula, but rather a declaration of whose authority we walk under.

> For apart from Me you can do nothing. — (John 15:5)

Without God involved, our lives are meaningless. When we attempt to make something of our lives, we end up coming around only to find them still empty. Unless God is involved, there is no worth. No matter how hard you try to be good or what you give, unless you are doing it with the Lord, it will be of no worth in the end. That's hard to imagine with so many charities and organizations helping others out. It's all well and good, but the Word is the Word, and if it says apart from God you can do nothing, then that's the end of the story.

> Truly, truly, I say to you, the Son can do nothing of Himself, unless it is something He sees the Father doing. — (John 5:19)

Jesus understood this. He knew that the only thing that mattered was what the Father was up to. He did as the Father asked, followed His example, and spread His name while on the earth. After three years of ministry, He died with 120 to His name. That's all. Of all the people healed, taught, and fed; only 120 were left together at the end. Yet those 120 went out, and in a short time the gospel had spread throughout the known world. Only God's planning could accomplish this. We too must move ourselves into the center of His will. As ambassadors of His name, we should reflect Him in all we do. To reach this point, we must abide in God.

> If you abide in Me, and My words abide in you, ask whatever you wish, and it will be done for you. My Father is glorified by this, that you bear much fruit, and so prove to be My disciples. Just as the Father has loved Me, I have also loved you; abide in My love. — (John 5:7–9)

God will answer our prayers not because we have used Jesus name, but because God loves us being like Jesus! We need only to abide in Him—staying in the Father's love. You see, it's nothing to do with what we do and everything to do with what God does.

> You did not choose Me but I chose you, and appointed you that you would go and bear fruit, and that your fruit would remain, so that whatever you ask of the Father in My name He may give to you. — (John 15:16)

His Glory

I have wondered many times why God has us pray. He knows what we need, He knows what's in our heart. Why then do we need to pray to Him? I finally ran across one of the reasons that God implemented prayer.

> Truly, truly, I say to you, he who believes in Me, the works that I do, he will do also; and greater works than these he will do; because I go to the Father. Whatever you ask in My name, that will I do, so that the Father may be glorified in the Son. If you ask Me anything in My name, I will do it. — (John 14:12–14)

These verses tell us that Jesus will answer our prayers so that the Father may be glorified. God's concern is not with how good we are, if we say the right words, or if we're important or not. He wants

His name and Jesus name to be glorified upon the earth. He wants everyone to come to know of His majesty.

> For Your name's sake You will lead me and guide me.
> — (Psalm 31:3)

Again, God will direct us to glorify His name. When people see the works He does for us in our lives, it reveals the truth of God's nature to them.

> You do not have because you do not ask. You ask and do not receive, because you ask with wrong motives, so that you may spend it on your pleasures. — (James 4:2–3)

Why are you asking? Are you asking for your comfort, selfishness, or ambition? Do you ask thinking only of yourself, or when you ask is it because what you are asking for that which will glorify God? Will your requests bring others to know Him and promote His kingdom upon the earth?

> This is the confidence which we have before Him, that, if we ask anything according to His will, He hears us. And if we know that He hears us in whatever we ask, we know that we have the requests which we have asked from Him. — (1 John 5:14–15)

It's the motive behind it all that is important. Are you trying to change God unto your will, or is your will changing to match God's? To say it a different way, we aren't trying to find God's will so that we can get our answers, but rather, we find His will so that we can help accomplish it.

He Is Still Faithful

> Now He was telling them a parable to show that at all times they ought to pray and not to lose heart, saying, "In a certain city there was a judge who did not fear God and did not respect man. There was a widow in that city, and she kept coming to him, saying, 'Give me legal protection from my opponent.' For a while he was unwilling; but afterward he said to himself, 'Even though I do not fear God nor respect man, yet because this widow bothers me, I will give her legal protection, otherwise by continually coming she will wear me out.'" And the Lord said, "Hear what the unrighteous judge said; now, will not God bring about justice for His elect who cry to Him day and night, and will He delay long over them? I tell you that He will bring about justice for them quickly." — (Luke 18:1–7)

For a long time, this scripture bothered me. We find a widow who needed legal protection and went to the judge. This judge didn't want to help her and repeatedly turned her away, but because her persistence was driving him crazy, he relented and gave her justice. This is followed by telling us how God will also provide justice. The lesson I typically heard preached from this passage would tell me that I needed to be persistent. If we ask and bother God long enough, He'll give us what we need. Is that not the impression you've gotten before? Probably not in those words of course, but that basic principle? I understand there are principles to standing firm, holding your ground, and not giving up, but even so the explanations I've heard often boil down to wearing God out by being annoying. At least, that was what I thought until God nudged me to take notice of the next verse in that passage.

> However, when the Son of Man comes, will He find faith on the earth? — (Luke 18:8)

What does that have to do with this passage? Initially, I was confused as to why it was asking if Jesus would find faith on this earth when He comes. What does that have to do with an unrighteous judge? After a bit, it dawned on me. Even though this judge was known as unrighteous, the widow had faith that he would give her justice in the end. Now for the million-dollar question. If this widow could have enough faith in an unrighteous judge to take care of her, why do we so easily give up on a righteous God when we haven't received an answer? He's not even like this judge that had to be badgered into doing what is right; God is good. Tell me then, do you have more faith in God to take care of you than this widow had in the unrighteous judge? Why is it that we stop bringing our prayers to Him when they aren't answered as quickly as we expect?

> Or what man is there among you who, when his son asks for a loaf, will give him a stone? Or if he asks for a fish, he will not give him a snake, will he? If you then, being evil, know how to give good gifts to your children, how much more will your Father who is in heaven give what is good to those who ask Him! In everything, therefore, treat people the same way you want them to treat you, for this is the Law and the Prophets. — (Matthew 7:9–12)

Have faith in God. He is our Father, the good shepherd. He will provide for us. Don't give up on His help so quickly when He doesn't answer like you wanted or takes too long. How many times as a child did you ask your parents for something and they wouldn't give it to you. Does it mean they didn't love you, or does it mean they cared so much they were willing to say no for your good? How often do you see parents give an answer to their kids, only to find that the child isn't mature enough to understand the reasoning? Sometimes they must be given the answer many times before they are mature enough to understand why. Sometimes the answer is even "because I said so." Believe that God wants to give you good things and that He wants you to understand why He does what He does. The problem is not with Him, but with us. We lose our faith in God because He doesn't seem to answer our prayers and it's just too hard for us to imagine the problem may be on our side. It amazes me that we can turn so quickly from our trust in God because of such small things. More likely the problem is our expectations. Let's go back and reread verse 7.

> Now, will not God bring about justice for His elect who cry to Him day and night, and will He delay long over them? — (Luke 18:7)

What is it Jesus said God would bring? Justice. He did not say He would bring comfort, material possessions, or wealth. He will bring justice. God will bring us what we deserve. Luckily, we're not talking about what we've earned, but what Jesus has bought for us. Find the promises in the Word, and pray in line with them. Start with who we are and what we've been promised.

Fear Not

Pray from your heart and not your mind. I have heard those who ask or command things to happen, and I have heard those who are so timid they are afraid to ask anything for fear they ask outside of God's will. Which way is correct? When I look at Jesus I see a little of both. The conclusion I have reached is that when I find myself analyzing how I should pray to get the right response, then I know I've stepped off course. I have ended up focusing more on the prayer than on the God I'm praying it to. This came to a head one day when I found myself wanting to pray, but couldn't even start because I didn't know the right way to ask God. That's when God spoke. His words were short and sweet as they often are to me. All He said was "I am your Father."

Don't pray like a politician who must guard every word so that nothing will be said wrong. God knows your heart anyway. Pray to a God who is your Father. Pray to a God who cares about you and knows what's best for you. Pray without restraint. You know what will happen if you do this? You'll begin to notice that your prayers will change into what you want them to be as you grow into the Lord. As you change, you'll understand more about God as you get to know Him better and pray more in line with Him. A prayer from the heart will never be wrong. Be bold in what you ask, but do not fear if it doesn't come to pass. God will not be angry because you have come to Him in a big way.

Consequently, we can't let a fear of failure stop us from trying. It's better to have tried and failed, then to have done nothing like the lukewarm church of Laodicea in Revelation 3. This is shown in our prayers as we use vague statements like "help us in our way", "let us remember you", or "help this person have strength". One of the phrases we use from our timidity is "if it be your will". I understand that Jesus prayed these very words, but keep in mind that when He prayed those words, Jesus knew the Father's will. He was so burdened with the path before Him, that He was hoping for another way. We, however, use it as a safety blanket. "God, heal this person, if it be your will." That way if they aren't healed, then we can say "oh, it must not have been God's will". We are concerned enough about what others might think if we ask for something and it doesn't happen, that we end up not asking for anything at all. We sound religious in our words, but I believe God would rather you be wrong and correct you, than for you to speak with empty words. Better a fire that burns too big than a timid spark that can be blown out with a simple breath.

Pray From The Heart

Some of us have been taught that emotions cannot be trusted and that they have no effect on our spiritual lives. This is wrong. Emotions can often distract or interfere with our walk, but they are also essential. Jesus said, "blessed are those who mourn", and Paul told one of the churches to "grieve, mourn and wail". Later Paul says he wants our "joy to be complete" and for us to have "joy unspeakable". The Christian life is not about ignoring our emotions, but harnessing and controlling them. Emotions have power behind them. Have you ever noticed how much more energy you get when you are either angry or happy? For example, my wife would sometimes fall asleep on the couch before we actually made it to bed. I would often attempt to wake her up and get her to bed. It seemed like she would be too tired to even move until I finally annoyed her so much that she would get mad. Suddenly, she had plenty of energy to make it to bed… and also to make other interesting comments about one particular husband who wouldn't stop bothering her. Anger that is directed and controlled gives us the resolve to fight our enemy. Repentance needs true spiritual grief if it is to turn our lives around. We need to have a joy flowing through us so that others can see the goodness of God. Sadness reveals a weakness where we need the Lord to touch our lives. As your emotions become purified you can even be led by them. God's emotions can flow through the Holy Spirit to our spirit and touch us. On multiple occasions we find that Jesus was first moved with compassion and then performed miracles.

When you pray, work on doing it with your heart and not just your mind. It's better to pray a prayer of questions and frustrations than one of platitudes. If you're praying with others, then you should somewhat censor your prayers so as not to break another's trust or to offend; however, when you're alone, God already knows what you're thinking. He knows what you feel. What's the point in guarding your tongue with him? If you're upset, pray that to the Lord. Be honest and truthful rather than trying to hide from Him as Adam and Eve did. You'll find that as you open up all of yourself before Him, God responds to our honesty and humility.

Prayer Is A Conversation

This next point is what I feel is one of the most important parts to prayer that I worry so many people don't understand or even believe.

The Jesus We Forgot

Our prayers to God are not one-way. It is too easy to find ourselves coming to God with only our requests. We may not even be selfish as these requests are often for others, yet our requests are not the only piece to prayer.

> Be anxious for nothing, but in everything by prayer and petition with thanksgiving let your requests be made known to God. — (Philippians 4:6)

This verse lists two ways we can come to God, by prayer and by petition. We petition God when we come asking Him for things, which means prayer is something else. Too often we don't make it past petition to actual prayer. The main purpose of prayer is not ourselves, but God. One of the keys to a dynamic prayer life is to understand that prayer is a two-way street. We're not the only ones with something to say. I mentioned this earlier, but I feel inclined to repeat this again as many times as I must to make sure you get it. You can hear God's voice.

> My sheep hear My voice, and I know them, and they follow Me. — (John 10:27)

> He who belongs to God hears what God says. The reason you do not hear is that you do not belong to God. — (John 8:47)

If this wasn't so clear in the Bible, I wouldn't be so blunt and honest about it. My personality wants me to tip-toe around this, since I believe there are so many people who don't hear God and this statement might upset or confuse them. I understand as most of my life has been the same as well. We have been spoon-fed truth and in many cases never learned to find it for ourselves. For that reason, some of us avoid or even build doctrines around not hearing directly from God. As I was working on this chapter I heard of a preacher in a good-sized church clearly say that you cannot hear God. His justification is that we have the Bible and don't need to hear God like they did back then. Fortunately, it doesn't need to be my word against his, for Jesus's words cut through all the silliness we can try to pile on it. Jesus was clear that if these people were of God, they would recognize His words as the words of God. We too can hear the words of God through the Spirit. God wants to speak to us today. Not just by magically flipping our Bibles to the right verse, but by Him speaking through our spirits to guide us and lead us into all truth. God can speak to us in many different ways if only we will listen.

Do you remember the time when Jesus saw some of the disciples coming in with their boat and He called out to them to put the nets down on the other side of the boat? After a day of failures, they didn't have to heed His word. These guys were fisherman by trade. They knew that just moving the nets wouldn't make a difference, but they went ahead and listened. That small act landed them a full net of fish. Imagine, if God can do that with fish, what could He do with men? If we can hear His voice and act on what He says, how much more will be accomplished in our lives? Few of us hear Him speaking often, but those that do can change lives by moving when God speaks.

An Audience

There's a comment I once heard about prayer that has long stuck with me. "Prayer is not a duty, but a delight." You are but one of billions of people who have been created by God, yet God Himself will reach down and speak to you. As this speaker described, you have an audience with the King. Imagine if you were able to walk up to the president to talk. In case you don't like the current president that much, pretend you had a chance to go up to Abraham Lincoln, George Washington, or another famous person you admire. Wouldn't that be an honor, to have some of their time devoted to you? How much more God? We take for granted the opportunity we have before us. When we come, it should be with such delight for the chance we have, such joy in the attention He gives, and such reverence at the

One we stand before. Yet all too often we make it a chore as we come before the throne of grace.

Getting Practical

<u>He will answer</u>
Let's look at what God tell us about our prayers.

> Call to Me and I will answer you, and I will tell you great and mighty things, which you do not know. — (Jeremiah 33:3)

His word says it right there. If we call to Him, He will answer. Now, in case you feel this verse could be out of context, here is another straight from Jesus.

> Ask, and it will be given to you; seek, and you will find; knock, and it will be opened to you. For everyone who asks receives, and he who seeks finds, and to him who knocks it will be opened. — (Matthew 7:7–8)

Everyone who asks. No concern on being out of context here. Ask, and we will receive. Believe in His Word. Believe also that our God is the good Father, wanting to watch over us. Bring your requests to Him, your troubles, your questions, and He will respond. It most likely won't immediately happen, and that is fine. Believe and stick at it like Daniel waiting for an answer. Do not give up. The enemy will fear when you truly wait upon God for an answer and will fight you. Just because you haven't heard doesn't mean you won't. If you haven't fought the fight, it may take time to begin hearing at all. Persevere.

Search for His will

> This is the confidence which we have before Him, that, if we ask anything according to His will, He hears us. And if we know that He hears us in whatever we ask, we know that we have the requests which we have asked from Him. — (1 John 5:14–15)

God is not a grocery store. We can't just come up and get whatever we want. He wants to give us good things, but obviously, that may not be the same as what we want. Have you ever considered that what happens upon the earth may be different than God's will? We know from His word that He desires all to be saved and yet we are told that many will follow the wide road to destruction. God wants a lot of things for us, but He will not force them to happen. God has given authority on earth to man, and it's up to us to make His will happen. This is the crux of asking in Jesus name. When we find His will, our prayers help bring the kingdom into the earth.

What does this mean for us? We need to seek His will. Just as Matthew said above, seek and you will find. Stand before God openly and ask for His guidance. Wait upon His mercies and seek after Him. He will respond and lead you.

Devote yourselves

> Devote yourselves to prayer, keeping alert in it with an attitude of thanksgiving. — (Colossians 4:2)

Remember, prayer is not a ritual. Prayer is not a play book we follow to get the things we need. Prayer is a conversation with our Father. Come to him like you would any other person. Don't recite a prayer like you would a school paper, but feel it like you would a note to a lover. Pour yourself into it. Don't just find time for prayer whenever you finish other things, make time for it. Set it aside from your day. Rise early, find a quiet room after the kids go down, or go out to your car during your lunch. It doesn't matter when or where, but that you set it aside, get alone with God, and devote your time to Him.

<u>Do not give up</u>

> Then He said to them, "Suppose one of you has a friend, and goes to him at midnight and says to him, 'Friend, lend me three loaves; for a friend of mine has come to me from a journey, and I have nothing to set before him'; and from inside he answers and says, 'Do not bother me; the door has already been shut and my children and I are in bed; I cannot get up and give you anything.' I tell you, even though he will not get up and give him anything because he is his friend, yet because of his persistence he will get up and give him as much as he needs. "So I say to you, ask, and it will be given to you; seek, and you will find; knock, and it will be opened to you. For everyone who asks, receives; and he who seeks, finds; and to him who knocks, it will be opened. Now suppose one of you fathers is asked by his son for a fish; he will not give him a snake instead of a fish, will he? Or if he is asked for an egg, he will not give him a scorpion, will he? If you then, being evil, know how to give good gifts to your children, how much more will your heavenly Father give the Holy Spirit to those who ask Him?
> — (Luke 11:5–13)

Like the parable of the unrighteous judge, Jesus again tells us to persist in asking. If God is good, how much more will He do whatever He can to help us and answer us? Too often we've used the fact that God has the power to do anything to justify our lack of faith when He doesn't do something. Just because God has the power, doesn't mean He can use it. Yes, you heard me right, there are some things God cannot do, if only for the fact that He has limited Himself. He set up laws that govern how this world works. There are laws of sowing and reaping, there is judgment for sin, and most especially there is free will. On top of this, God has a plan which He won't violate just to make you happy. This means that since He is good, there will be times He cannot do what we want even though it may seem good to us. It's not just that He chooses not to, but that if He did, it would violate Himself.

> If we are faithless, He remains faithful, for He cannot deny Himself. — (2 Timothy 2:13)

Do not give up. I cannot stress the important of this. Some things are too important to receive unless you've proven your dedication. Moses wanted to free his fellow Israelites but had to wait for 40 years before He was ready for God to use him. In other instances of our lives, God's answers for us can be blocked by the enemy. Daniel had one prayer answered in minutes, but in another case persisted in prayer for weeks before getting an answer. Often, we find that our time spent in prayer is not changing God's will to answer us, but changing our hearts to receive it. There is nothing more effective than finding God's will in accomplishing His work, and most likely nothing more contested by the enemy either.

Pray continually

> Rejoice always; pray without ceasing; in everything give thanks; for this is God's will for you in Christ Jesus. — (1 Thessalonians 5:16–18)

What does "pray without ceasing" mean? The obvious interpretation is that I should always be in prayer with the Lord. I'm not sure if you've tried that, but for me it typically didn't work out well. My job requires deep concentration, so I don't think it's even possible for me to be praying while doing much of my work. Yet the words are here, so like I've said before, I believe the Bible over my experience. For this reason, I would keep trying on and off over the years? After some time, God revealed a truth in this verse through a message I heard a few years back. It just took a while to sink in. This preacher believed the translators didn't get the wording right from his viewpoint. I went looking up the Greek word for myself and guess what I found out?

I don't know Greek.

But once I got past that, I found the roots of the word and what they meant, and I can see his point. The word for "without ceasing" could also be translated as "at the proper time". We aren't to always pray, but rather always be ready to pray. We don't know when the Lord will come upon our hearts with someone who needs intercession, with an opportunity before us, or even when He just wants to talk. I have found He decides to talk at times when I don't expect.

Here's what I try to do. I need to work on other things, and I can't split my attention between that and God, as it's not fair to either. Instead, I just start with God. Much like giving where you set the first fruits aside, I start the day in the morning by talking with Him. Then as I need to move to different tasks, I take my leave. If I feel that our time isn't done—that He's trying to show me something and I shouldn't move on—then I don't. What that can do is make me late to work, take a little time from work in between things, force me to hold off on meals, or stop me from doing other tasks. The way I see it, God knows what's happening better than me. I'm a better worker if I'm walking in God's presence than if I'm not. I'm a better husband if I'm listening to the Lord than if I'm not. I'm happier abiding in Him than abiding in myself.

My life becomes part of my prayer. I do the work that needs done to glorify God, then to my family to rejoice in them as a gift from Him. As I wake, I thank Him for the day, and I ask what He is doing today. If there is no answer, I ask Him to help me see it as I walk. I work hard to honor Him with the gifts He's given. My life becomes an act of worship to Him. Most importantly, I wait on the

Lord. I don't want to force prayer upon Him in my timeframes. If I feel there's something we need to discuss, I take some time then to talk. I don't put other things above our relationship. I don't try to squeeze God into the role I've made for Him, rather I put Him first, then let the other things fall around Him. This is one of the biggest mistakes we as Christians often make. We have this desire for God, but then we try to fit Him into our schedule. Want to know a secret? He doesn't fit. We fit into Him.

> Rest in the Lord and wait patiently for Him — (Psalm 37:7)

Wait for God to move first. Don't go charging off into everything that seems right, rather wait patiently for the Lord.

> For apart from Me(Jesus) you can do nothing — (John 15:5)

Wait on the Lord

Eyes To See

> There was the true Light which, coming into the world, enlightens every man. He was in the world, and the world was made through Him, and the world did not know Him. — (John 1:9-10)

This verse weighs heavily upon me. Jesus came into a world made through Him, but the world did not recognize Him. He walked among a people formed by His hands and they missed it. Is this verse true of us as well? If Jesus were to walk through our world, would we recognize Him for who He is?

Be honest.

Let's step back to His birth and look there. The law and the prophets had been pointing toward a savior coming since the beginning. The Jewish people have listened to the prophecies and looked toward the coming of their messiah. Then one day, the Word of God became flesh. His hospital was a stable, His audience was a group of shepherds, and His first outfit a mere cloth. After the Son of God was born, we see only a small number who noticed. All of heaven stood at attention watching as the Holy One came to earth as a man, yet mankind nearly missed it. This sort of thing grieves my heart, and I hope it does yours as well. How much do you think it hurt God that so few would even notice His child being born?

The shepherds were perhaps the first to notice. As far as we know, they weren't looking for any signs, just watching their sheep. Bethlehem was packed with people for the census, but in the end the angels came to the shepherds. Why is it that they were chosen? Was it to make a statement that this Messiah is available to all, even to the lowly shepherds? Maybe a sign that Jesus would be the great shepherd? Was it because they would have the open heart to believe and go see? Or perhaps was it simply because they were only ones available to receive a word from God? It could be any or all of these reasons, yet in my heart I believe they were chosen because they were available. How many others do you suppose the angels passed over that didn't notice? Next on the scene were the wise men.

> Now after Jesus was born in Bethlehem of Judea in the days of Herod the king, magi from the east arrived in Jerusalem, saying, "Where is He who has been born King of the Jews? For we saw His star in the east and have come to worship Him." — (Matthew 2:1–2)

We know so little about these Magi, but one thing we do know—they were watching. Not only were they available to hear from God, they were actively watching for signs of God moving. These Magi saw the truth in the stars, followed it, and glorified God for His greatness. Wise enough to see the signs, brave enough to follow them. Then we come to Simeon.

> And there was a man in Jerusalem whose name was Simeon; and this man was righteous and devout, looking for the consolation of Israel; and the Holy Spirit was upon him. And it had been revealed to him by the Holy Spirit that he would not see death before he had seen the Lord's Christ. — (Luke 2:25-26)

What an amazing description for a man, to be known as righteous and devout! What a gift to have the Holy Spirit confide in you such a mystery of God. Here was a man who had spent much of his life on his knees before God: trusting in Him, following His precepts, and waiting for our salvation to come. Few men find the truth of God and spend their lives standing upon it. Still, there was another at the temple as well.

> And there was a prophetess, Anna the daughter of Phanuel, of the tribe of Asher. She was advanced in years and had lived with her husband seven years after her marriage, and then as a widow to the age of eighty-four. She never left the temple, serving night and day with fastings and prayers. At that very moment she came up and began giving thanks to God, and continued to speak of Him to all those who were looking for the redemption of Jerusalem.
> — (Luke 2:36–37)

How long do you think Anna lived in the temple praying? Over time I have come to look forward to my times with God, to that alone time for us to talk and to pour myself out to Him, yet, I don't last long. Most of us speak of that time in minutes, some of us in hours, but for Anna, that was years. If she were to marry at a typical age, then she probably spent at least 50 years in the temple praying. To me that speaks of an intimacy I could only ever hope for. We don't know if Anna had been told ahead of time that Jesus was coming, but she sure knew when to show up. She was in tune with God at a level that she knew something was going on. As Luke said, "at that very moment she came up." It's as if she was praying and God pointed out Jesus to her saying: "there I am."

Were Jesus to show up in our midst, would we notice. If He began touching people's hearts and changing lives around us, would we see past our own lives to take notice? To wait upon the Lord is to be ready. Not only must you be listening and watching, but have the time to react as well. Be as available as the shepherds, as observant as the magi, as devout as Simeon, and as dedicated as Anna. Waiting upon God is to give Him the first chance with your life and to not overlook Him.

Rushing Is Not Trusting

The first step is to stop rushing. Whether for good or bad reasons, we have a tendency to take what little we know and try to run out and live it. Zealousness can lead to mistakes just as quickly as timidity. Abraham attempted to rush God's plan, and he bore Ishmael, whom many consider to be one of the fathers of Islam. Moses attempted to rush freedom for his people and found himself exiled for 40 years before finally returning to lead the Israelites out of Egypt. In contrast, when we come to Jesus we find a different story. We see very little of Jesus's life before He was thirty; yet in one passage we find him at age twelve and able to amaze the teachers of the law with His understanding. Even so, He didn't start His ministry until age 30. What do you suspect He was doing all that time? He was preparing for the right time. He was waiting on God.

> Yet those who wait for the Lord will gain new strength.
> — (Isaiah 40:31)

God has much preordained for us. He's been working to prepare us for the tasks in our path from before we were born. If we jump ahead of Him, we'll find ourselves unfit for what is to come. In His time, He provides us the strength to follow through with our lives. If we are willing to wait upon His timing, we'll find better results than we could accomplish on our own and the strength to accomplish it.

As I am writing this particular section, I can say that I have been in one of those periods. I had been waiting on something more from the Lord. He had given me many revelations that have turned into much of this book, but I only had pieces of the puzzle, not the whole picture. Looking back, I find that I have been slowly putting this book together for almost 10 years now. As it is, I've been waiting for the Lord to say "go". I will continue to work on it, slowly putting pieces together, as I wait for the Lord to put His stamp of approval on my work. Until that occurs, this will only be a bunch of words on my computer. I will continue to write, and more especially continue to seek revelation from the Lord, but I would not dare to set this out until I feel the call. Godly timing and direction are worth more than all the talent and work I can put in. It's only now, after all this time, that I have begun to feel the confidence that the Lord is moving this work ahead.

> Rest in the Lord and wait patiently for Him; do not fret because of him who prospers in his way, because of the man who carries out wicked schemes. Cease from anger and forsake wrath; do not fret; it leads only to evildoing. For evildoers will be cut off, but those who wait for the Lord, they will inherit the land. — (Psalm 37:7–9)

God needs time to change us, to prepare us for what He has in store. Be careful, however, not to mistake the church's calling for God's calling. Churches need people to serve. There are always ministries in need of more hands to do their work, yet that ministry is not necessarily God's ministry. Don't get me wrong. I am not saying to refuse to volunteer in your church when they need help. God loves our service. I am speaking more of God's call on your life and the area you can serve Him best. You need to wait upon the Lord. If you are at a point where you know God has more for you, but you're feeling confused as to what you should be doing for the Lord, then you need to focus upon Him. Don't continue living your life hoping to figure it out some day, but take it to the Lord. Spend time with Him each day and listen for Him to speak. I'm not speaking of a quiet time either, that's a given. You need to spend more time with your Lord, looking for Him, listening for Him, and preparing yourself for His moving. Don't let life consume your time where you don't find the life God has planned for you.

Finding God's will for our lives is perhaps the most important thing we could do. I am amazed at how few people truly want to know the will of God. If you were to ask a Bible study or Sunday school class if they want to know God's will for their life, most or all of the members would raise their hand. If you then ask that same group how many have fasted in the last 6 months, how many hands would be raised? Our mouths say we want to know His will, but our actions say otherwise. There are so few Christians who will lay their life aside and seek the Lord until they know. This surprises me. Why do we live our lives unsure if we are going in the right direction? There will be periods of waiting, dryness, and even silence, but God desires to reveal His will. Sometimes His word may be to just "keep going", but even that is direction. When Daniel found a scripture that gave him hope for his nation, he fasted for 21 days while waiting for an answer. How far are we willing to go?

Waiting upon the Lord is acknowledging that our life isn't complete in itself, so we will stand near and wait until He's ready to lead us into the life He's prepared. We need to come to know better than to make our own judgments. The Lord sees our level of commitment and the desire of our heart, and rewards us for this.

Attend To Him

Those who wait upon the Lord are ready for any task He gives. We find them more than able to accomplish His will. They have purposed themselves to do the Lord's will, spent the time to be prepared, and are waiting in their place for what is to come. Jesus spoke of these servants:

> Who then is the faithful and sensible slave whom his master put in charge of his household to give them their food at the proper time? Blessed is that slave whom his master finds so doing when he comes —
> (Matthew 24:45–46)

These servants have proven themselves faithful and are able to take on much more. The best metaphor I can think of is actually a waiter in a restaurant. The good ones are always on the lookout, always ready to get what you need. They show up with refills before you ask and quickly bring you the food when it's prepared. They know the menu and are ready to answer your questions. In essence, they take care of your needs. We also should be diligent for the Lord, for His needs. What can we do to please Him, to provide for what He is doing? Yet to do this, we must first learn how.

Draw Near

> Draw near to God and He will draw near to you. — (James 4:8)

Again I will repeat, you're as close to God as you want to be. Those who can be honest with themselves will understand this statement. We know that we make choices for ourselves over God all the time. Whether it's a movie instead of a quiet time or a sin instead of obedience. God has given us more than enough opportunities to draw closer to Him. To truly wait upon God, we need more than a desire.

> 'For I know the plans that I have for you,' declares the Lord, 'plans for welfare and not for calamity to give you a future and a hope. 'Then you will call upon Me and come and pray to Me, and I will listen to you. 'You will seek Me and <u>find Me</u> when you search for Me with all your heart. 'I will be found by you,' declares the Lord. — (Jeremiah 29:11–14)

This verse is often quoted to remind us that God has a plan in store for us. I'm excited about that. I love that God has put something together for me; that His hand is upon me and He has set a work ahead of me to accomplish. Bearing that in mind, the next part of the passage promised something better. I can find Him. I am joyful over this in accordance with my view of finding God. I don't substitute salvation for finding God. No, I'm excited because I can encounter God in a very real way. If I bring my whole heart and being into it, I can find God. Not a feeling, goose bumps, or a calm peaceful warmth, but God Himself can be found and known.

Bread Of His Presence

> You shall make a table of acacia wood, two cubits long and one cubit wide and one and a half cubits high. You shall overlay it with pure gold and make a gold border around it... You shall set the bread of the Presence on the table before Me at all times. — (Exodus 25:23–24,30)

"At all times." Those words were my clue that I needed to stop and think about this scripture. Why would God require fresh bread to be in His temple all the times, unless it were to convey a message? What could be so important? When the Israelites were wandering in the dessert, God gave them manna to sustain them. That manna was also referred to as bread from heaven. Simply, bread is the substance that sustains and strengthens us. The bread in the temple was the bread of God's presence. It seems to symbolize that the presence of God is what will sustain us and provide for us. There are patterns we can find in scripture. One of them is that when the presence of God left Israel, they fell quickly. When He was with them, they stood against all odds. The person that comes to my mind first, when I think about the presence of God, is Moses. Who else has stood in the cloud of His presence, witnessed His form pass by, and was so marked by being in His presence that his face shown with the glory? My favorite scripture concerning Moses is in Exodus 33. The context here is that Israel had created a golden calf to worship while Moses was up on the mountain receiving the ten commandments. When he came down, he found the calf and punished the Israelites for it. After this, Moses went aside to petition God on their behalf, knowing what God's anger would be like. Once Moses had convinced God to spare the Israelites—which is above my understanding that God's mind could be changed by Moses— the Lord responded to Moses with this statement.

> Then the LORD spoke to Moses, "Depart, go up from here, you and the people whom you have brought up from the land of Egypt, to the land of which I swore to Abraham, Isaac, and Jacob, saying, 'To your descendants I will give it.' I will send an angel before you and I will drive out the Canaanite, the Amorite, the Hittite, the Perizzite, the Hivite and the Jebusite. Go up to a land flowing with milk and honey; for I will not go up in your midst, because you are an obstinate people, and I might destroy you on the way."
> — (Exodus 33:1–3)

We find here a different kind of mercy from the Lord. He was within His right to destroy them and start over if wanted, yet He chose to continue helping them. He would send His angel before them to clear the way, but the Lord did not want to go with them, as He knew that they would turn away from Him again and again. In their continual rebellion, He feared that He would grow weary and destroy them. His mercy was to remove Himself, yet still provide what they needed. Sounds like much of my life, provided, but not anointed. Had I been there, I probably would've grieved and taken it. You see, if I'm upsetting God that much, maybe it's better for a little time apart. We do that in our friendships, work relationships, and marriages; why not with God. Moses, however, wasn't willing to take this path.

> Then he said to Him, "If Your presence does not go with us, do not lead us up from here." — (Exodus 33:15)

Moses knew something that I wouldn't have known. He understood that without the presence of God, they might as well just stop where they were. Israel was special because the Lord was walking with them. That presence defined them and set them apart. They couldn't be what they were meant to be without His presence.

As we continue with the story of Moses, we come across his servant Joshua.

> Whenever Moses entered the tent, the pillar of cloud would descend and stand at the entrance of the tent; and the LORD would speak with Moses. When all the people saw the pillar of cloud standing at the entrance of the tent, all the people would arise and worship, each at the entrance of his tent. Thus the LORD used to speak to Moses face to face, just as a man speaks to his friend. When Moses returned to the camp, his servant Joshua, the son of Nun, a young man, would not depart from the tent. — (Exodus 33:9–11)

After Moses would leave the tent where God's glory came down, he would head back to camp, but Joshua would stay. Joshua did not stay for anyone else; he stayed for God. Moses often was meeting with God to get answers, find direction, and provide for Israel, but afterward, Joshua stayed for the presence. When Moses would move on, Joshua would linger. I'm not saying Joshua was better than Moses, for he was not at the level of relationship that Moses had with the Lord, but he yearned to stay in the presence. He had a revelation that few of us do. As the Psalmist declared:

> Better is one day in your courts than a thousand elsewhere. — (Psalm 84:10)

Do you live in the presence of the Lord? How about when you can feel Him in the church after worship or a service? How often do you see people just staying in God's house to be with Him? In our town we have a prayer room one of the local churches supports. It's a place you can come and just spend time in prayer. I drive past it often and there are rarely many people there. Similarly, our church occasionally starts up prayer meetings. They don't last long. Then we wonder why we feel so little from God? When was the last time you found a quiet place, put aside your Bible and your prayer lists, and just sat with the Lord. Do you hear His voice in the stillness? Do you find strength from focusing upon Him? If you don't, then perhaps you should start. As it is, when we feel the Lord moving in our hearts, we are quick to act rather than sitting in His presence.

> I am the living bread that came down out of heaven; if anyone eats of this bread, he will live forever; and the bread also which I will give for the life of the world is My flesh. — (John 6:51)

As so much of scripture does, we find bread pointing back to Jesus. He is the Word come down from heaven. He is the Living Word, the completion of the written Word. What says presence more than Immanuel himself? Jesus brought the very essence of the Father with Him, giving us all a glimpse into His heart. As He walked the earth, so did God. How do we find the presence? By finding Jesus.

> And surely I am with you always, to the very end of the age. — (Matthew 28:20)

Begin to practice this verse. Jesus is here with us at all times. If we keep in mind that He is always with us, then He's seeing what we're doing and listening to what we're saying. For that reason, we should act in a way that will honor Him, because He's there with us. We start there, but move on to feeling His presence and His presence being with us. There's a well-known book that covers this concept, it's called "Practicing His Presence" by Brother Lawerence. He was a 17th century monk who was known for his walk with the Lord. He accredited so much to a practice of the presence of God. In his every moment he would try to keep his mind upon the Lord. He would worship the Lord, focusing upon Him, talking to Him, and mostly just loving Him. If you are interested, I'd recommend reading his book. He reached a place in his relationship that he was always surrounded or filled by the love of God. He could feel His presence as he made meals, worked in the garden, or did any number of other chores. His life because a song of worship to God, and it flowed out of him to everyone he met. As you make progress here you will find things easier to do, the presence closer and closer, until one day when that great mystery happens, and you find "Christ in you, the hope of glory" (Colossians 1:27).

The Practice Of Waiting

As with many other spiritual disciplines, there is a lifestyle and a practice. You live a lifestyle of prayer, but then you set apart time to focus and pray. You live a life of worship by the actions you take, and then you step aside to worship God with all your attention. You live a lifestyle of waiting upon the Lord, and you also step aside to solely wait in His presence.

Be still and know that I am God — (Psalm 46:10)

The process of becoming still is a lot of work for us these days. It may seem odd to say that being still is work, yet there it is. Remember that exercise we did earlier where I asked you to focus solely upon the Lord? Our minds and souls are so cluttered with this world, that we can barely stop to think straight. How can you be quiet and still before the Lord if you're always thinking about work, family, that next show, the movie coming out next week, hunting season starting, the friend who said something mean, etc. Even more, most of us tend to lead such busy lives between work, family, friends, entertainment, and events that we cannot find time to sit still and be quiet. Music and books can even be a danger here when we fill every free moment we have by shoving more things into our mind.

Often, we will only hear God's voice from our rest, so we must learn to become still that we may distinguish His voice from our own mental turmoil. The busier your mind is, the harder it is for the Lord to reach you. Think of it as being in a crowded area. It's hard to pick out a single voice talking when there are 20 other conversations going on. Now imagine that person is somewhere out of sight and talking. Unless you're ready for it and listening, you'd miss it. This is even tougher if you don't know that person's voice well. It is the same with God. Early on we just have no other method than to be still and quiet so we may hear Him. As we learn the sound of His voice, it can become easier to distinguish Him from the noise.

> For thus the Lord God, the Holy One of Israel, has said, "In repentance and rest you will be saved, In quietness and trust is your strength." — (Isaiah 30:15)

Unfortunately, many of us stay busy for a reason we often don't want to admit to ourselves. We're just unhappy. This is the truth I finally came to realize about myself. If I stopped doing things, I found out that I didn't like the life I was living, I wasn't content with who I was, and I didn't know what to do with myself. We have become so superficial with our lives that there's no depth to fall back on and find ourselves. These people can be found all around us. They don't have the self-confidence in who they are to not be doing something. For some, it's work. They throw their lives into their work with abandon, and when asked, they're quick to define themselves as what their occupation is. They get satisfaction and pride out of what they do, associating themselves with that. For others, they turn to friends. They want to be with others all the time, most often so they don't have to think for themselves. This next one is a dangerous one to even mention, but for some it's family. There are many parents who identify themselves by their children. They spend their lives before having children thinking that kids will make them happy. They jump in and have kids quickly, often to find themselves going through the motions with no heart. It's especially evident when the kids move out and the parents can't recover their lives. Don't get discouraged if I'm calling you out, as I have called myself out as well. Treating the symptoms won't fix the problem. We need to get to the root of the problem. We need to come to the point we find our identity and confidence in the Lord. To do this, we get alone with Him and work it out. David tells us the first step for entering into His presence.

> Enter His gates with thanksgiving, and His courts with praise. — (Psalm 100:4)

If you want to wait upon the Lord, first you must draw near. When you are coming into His presence, you should lead with thanksgiving and praise. I don't know if this verse tells us that our natural response of coming into His presence is to praise, or that praise is the entrance into His presence. Either way, thanksgiving and praise are an integral part of drawing near to God. To be clear, I'm not saying to throw in your worship CD in your car and sing along with it, I'm talking honest praise.

> And do not get drunk with wine, for that is dissipation, but be filled with the Spirit, speaking to one another in psalms and hymns and spiritual songs, singing and making melody with your heart to the Lord; always giving thanks for all things in the name of our Lord Jesus Christ to God, even the Father. — (Ephesians 5:18–20)

Make melody with your heart. Sometimes I would try to force it by putting on a praise song to get myself "in the mood," so I can walk in the spirit. To be honest, this doesn't usually work out for me. It takes a desire, humility, and willingness to empty yourself. We must be humble enough to be open and honest. To come before God admitting we can't do it and to cry for His help. Instead, we follow the routine that makes us comfortable and find ourselves admitted closer to our "comfortable" idol. You cannot worship on a timetable. You lift your voice and heart up to God, praise Him for what He's done, worship Him for who He is. As your soul comes into unity with your spirit you can begin to enter into that presence.

Next you need to get still. You will have to make a plan here. You can't just look for time when you have it; you must make time. For me it's early morning or late evening when my daughter is asleep. Go to a place by yourself, find a comfortable position where you won't fall asleep, and sit. Oddly, the position can be important, especially as you stay silent, because as you get still you might just find yourself nodding off. Be comfortable so that you're not distracted by your body, but not enough that you can fall asleep. For me this means not resting my head on something. Once you're there, just keep sitting. This is not your typical quiet time where you follow your reading plan, break out your journal, and do the five steps of prayer. This isn't a time to come to God with your prayer list either. There is another time for that. First you come to the Lord and praise Him. Then set your mind upon the Lord and stay there; whether it's a loving conversation, silent adoration, or just a simple visualization. Spend some time there, try to keep your mind open, and listen. Then do it again. And again. There's a time for prayer, a time for Bible reading, and a time to just wait.

Time is one of the keys here. Anything less involves us trying to do what we can to get what we want. When you hear someone giving you certain amounts of time you should be praying or reading your Bible, beware a religious spirit. There is no formula for being close to God, and when you're talking about a relationship, there is no substitute for time. Dating should've taught us that. There are no shortcuts in a relationship. Take the time to be with the Lord. Let me be clear here as I was missing this for so long. God will of course meet you where you are and He understands those who have an excess of time verses those with only a little. Even so, I find I can't be still in a matter of minutes. Especially early on, you cannot quiet yourself down in five minutes. What I've often heard is that it takes 30 minutes to an hour for those who are new to this to become still. Practice makes it easier, but you need to find times where you can devote a significant amount of time to the Lord.

> Rejoicing in hope, persevering in tribulation, devoted
> to prayer — (Romans 12:12)

This verse contains a key word for us—devoted. That really says it all. Not praying often or for long periods of time. Devoted. You are setting aside time, putting this in front of other things. It's important and premeditated, not just something you do if there's a chance. It's planned and consistent. You don't need to get legalistic and have a set amount of time every day. It should just be a habit you form. My best measure is when I'm doing it more times than I'm not. Whenever you find yourself asking questions like "how long should I be praying", "should I read through the Bible in a year or chapter at a time", or "should I journal every day", you should stop and reassess if you are off track. Whenever you're looking at trying to find a certain method or a certain way to do something, there's a danger you're headed toward idolatry or religion. Religion tells us that if I add these things together and put the ingredients just right, I get this as a result. Our religious behaviors tell us that if we say the right prayer often enough, then God will do what we want. Have you noticed this? By contrast, when you're in a relationship and focused on what God is doing and just wanting to be with Him, then when the chance comes your way to find time with God, you take it. Rather than forcing a set time, where things interfere, you can flow as God does. Discipline is good, but not at the cost of relationship.

> You will keep him in perfect peace, whose mind is stayed on you: because he trusts in you. — (Isaiah 26:3)

I spoke before about the practice of His presence. As you wait, you focus your mind upon the Lord. To do this well, you should make this a habit at all times, always bringing your mind back to the Lord. It draws you nearer, but also brings you peace. Peace to know what is important and who is there for you. Keep your mind upon God. When you wait, say His name, picture Him, and just love Him. Love is important above all us. If you wait upon Him, but don't love Him, it's all a waste.

Jesus answered and said to him, "If any one loves Me, he will keep My word; and My Father will love him, and We will come to him and make Our abode with him. — (John 14:23)

Testing of Faith

Are You Satisfied With Your Life?

It's a fair question. Looking around, I see a lot of unhappy people. We do like to complain and argue. We gripe about how life is unfair, complain about the things people have done to us, and continue on about what we deserve. To be honest, most of us are dissatisfied. We see our lives and don't like what we find ourselves going through, typically believing that we deserve better. Dissatisfaction is rooted in our expectations. Instead of seeing all our blessings as gifts, we've come to expect certain gifts as what we deserve. Then when we don't receive them, we become upset. Especially in the western world, we tend to feel like we are entitled to more. We've grown up and been provided so much that we believe it's what we deserve. We deserve to be fed, own a house, drive a car, have a job, and have friends to share it with. When we don't get those things, we blame others for taking away what we should have. When we come upon hard times, we believe that we don't deserve them. Let me give you two stories to demonstrate.

First, let's talk about me. When my daughter was born, my wife and I figured out pretty quickly that we weren't naturals at this whole parenting thing. It took me a while, but I've come to the belief that we do a good job, it's just that our good job seems to be harder for us than most. I'm guessing most people probably feel this way. Our fun started early. Because of some small complications during the birth, we stayed a second night at the hospital. Since we were new parents, we were happy for a little more help that second night as we try to adjust to this whole new world of parenthood. About an hour after the nurses take our daughter to the nursery for the night, they show back up, handed our daughter back, and told us that "she's crying too much." This is where we looked at each other in a little bit of shock.

We've been down to the nursery and there were always babies crying. That's just what they do. So somehow our baby was so much worse than the rest, that the nurses couldn't handle her and brought her back. We knew we were in trouble then, which began our four month stint of severe colic. I would like to say we handled it well, but we didn't. We had a lot of questions for each other, our doctor, and even God. We wondered what we did to deserve this and how we could fix it. If you've had a colicky child, you will understand. If you haven't, just imagine that you have a baby that would only do 3 things: eat, sleep, or cry. That was our life for four months. I nearly cried the day she decided she would hang out in the baby swing for five minutes without crying. Yes, you read that correctly, five minutes. You have no idea how much I can get done in five minutes when I had two hands free. Keep in mind, we have no experience with babies, and we were pretty much left alone to figure it out (I think this was somewhat our doing). We had times where we came to the end of ourselves. After about two months of everyone unhappy, I got to the point where I wanted to just give up. For a while I sought God more, then finally I just stopped. I retreated into a place where I just tried to survive. I didn't enjoy, I didn't excel, I just tried to tread water and not do something stupid. Remember that verse that comes after putting on the armor of God, "and after you have done everything, to stand" (Ephesians 6:13)? That was pretty much me.

A couple months later we hear the story of a couple in our area with their own challenge. Search for "99 balloons" on the internet and you'll find their story. Here's the quick rundown: their son was born with an underdeveloped lung, a heart with a hole in it, and a DNA problem. I don't remember all the details, and for our purposes here, they're not required. The important detail is that the doctors told them he would not survive. This is how they began their parenthood. Each day was a miracle to them. Every day they would have a birthday party to celebrate another day with their child. I would love to go into more detail, but wouldn't give it the credit it's due. If you're curious, watch their video. At each birthday, they had a balloon. After 99 days, their son passed away, hence the name

"99 balloons". The joy and love that came from them was amazing. Their faith let them enjoy the little time that they had, whereas my faith could barely hold me up in such a less challenging situation. We have a choice as to how we approach our life. We can continue to approach life as what we've earned, only to become disappointed about everything we lose, or we can approach life as a gift. Each day is another gift from God that we didn't deserve. That's why it's called a gift. For this reason, we take each day, each moment, and treasure it for what it is. When it goes away, we are glad for the chance to have experienced it. We thank God for the opportunities He's given us.

Stand Under Trial

> Therefore, take up the full armor of God, so that you will be able to resist in the evil day, and having done everything, to stand firm. — (Ephesians 6:13)

How long do you stand? Do you stand under the trial for a while and finally give in like me? I find myself in a tough position, and do my best to hang on, only to give out. For a while my trials drew me closer to God, leading me to prayer, knowing that I needed His help and only His help to do it. Finally, I just couldn't go farther. The stress, fatigue, and ...well... despair finally caught up. I just gave up for a little while. I didn't fall away, but for a while the Lord just had to carry me. I look back on that period and wonder what would happen if I had kept strong. I wonder how much more strength I would have if I had carried myself through with godly faith.

Where do you go when your faith is tested? When you find yourself overwhelmed at work, hounded by your spouse, getting angry at your kids, and somehow messing up everything you put your hands on; where do you go? Do you run away? I know some people that literally do that. They will leave for days at a time and just sleep in a car or hotel room, then once they're over whatever happened to them they show back up. I tend to run away in my head. I would retreat emotionally, bury myself in books, and generally try to think of anything other than the life I am living. I have also seen others bury themselves in self-pity, letting everyone around them know how difficult their life is and how small all your problems are compared to theirs. Now let's compare these examples to David.

> Moreover David was greatly distressed because the people spoke of stoning him, for all the people were embittered, each one because of his sons and his daughters. But David strengthened himself in the Lord his God. — (1 Samuel 30:6)

David looked to the Lord and found the strength to bear his trials. I like how it says he "strengthened himself in the Lord." This was something that David chose to do. David stepped aside in his trial and found the strength in God to continue on in faith.

> For consider Him who has endured such hostility by sinners against Himself, so that you will not grow weary and lose heart. — (Hebrews 12:3)

We often don't take the time to just step aside and to look at where we are. The ability to step back from your problems and change your point of view is necessary for your growth. Look at what is important and not just what the issue is.

Reward At The End Of Trials

> Therefore, do not throw away your confidence, which has a great reward. For you have need of endurance, so that when you have done the will of God, you may receive what was promised. — (Hebrews 10:35)

Giving up is more of a loss than we realize because there is a great reward at the end of the trial for those who hold firm. If we've held firm through something and have kept our eyes open and our wits about us, then we can lead others through the same wilderness. We should also look at trials as exercise. If we can make it through, we will find not only more strength, but more confidence. God allows difficulties into our lives as preparation. Like weights, we start small, and work our way up. God has great things for us, but great trials may come as well. We need to be ready to handle them, and our path to larger opportunities is to build our strength in smaller ones. Don't waste your sorrows. We know God sets trials in our path. If we wish to move on in God, we must move on through them. If we don't pass, God takes us around and we come back to try again. Hopefully we won't need to go through them too many times before learning our lesson.

> In this you greatly rejoice, even though now for a little while, if necessary, you have been distressed by various trials, so that the proof of your faith, being more precious than gold which is perishable, even though tested by fire, may be found to result in praise and glory and honor at the revelation of Jesus Christ. — (1 Peter 1:6–7)

Power Perfected

> And He has said to me, "My grace is sufficient for you, for power is perfected in weakness." Most gladly, therefore, I will rather boast about my weaknesses, so that the power of Christ may dwell in me. — (2 Corinthians 12:9)

Another truth we should embrace is that our weaknesses brings more of Christ in us. Through our trials, we show more of Him to those around us. I love how the scripture says that His power is perfected in us. It's simple enough. If we had the ability to face this world with our strength, how would that glorify God? If we could stand under a trial based only on our knowledge, what is there for others to acknowledge except us. God wants the glory, which is fair enough as it's all His to begin with. For this reason, when we face something that we cannot do ourselves, it's giving God the opportunity to show His greatness.

> For we do not have a high priest who cannot sympathize with our weaknesses, but One who has been tempted in all things as we are, yet without sin.
> — (Hebrews 4:15)

Jesus has stood under all things, and He knows our weaknesses. He was a man as well. When you are tested, find faith in knowing that Jesus stood under the same tests as you, and the same grace that He had is now sufficient for you. You are not alone. The enemy will attempt to make you feel alone and believe that no one understands what you are going through, but Jesus is always with you encouraging and strengthening. Trust in His Word.

Why Must I Be Tested?

Inevitably, our struggles will lead us to question why. Let's go back over the reasons that we've mentioned here.

- We are tested to show his glory. The greatness of God is shown as we walk through trials we could not handle ourselves. One of the jobs of a disciple is to show God's glory to the rest of the world. Not only can the world see it, but we see it ourselves. When we can handle something that others could not, we show God.
- Tests build our reliance upon Him. Pride is always an enemy. When we begin to think we can do it ourselves is the time when Satan can sneak in and lead us away. Humility is an important key to walking in God. Weaknesses lead us to lean upon the Lord, to trust in Him and find our strength through

Him. As Jesus said, "apart from me you can do nothing" (John 15:5).
- Tests are there for our growth. As God provides and works us through one trial, we are strengthened by this to handle others. As we learn to walk in one level, we can be moved to another and promoted.

Trials show us that God's grace is sufficient. We need to understand that God knows what is best for us and has given us what we need. We need to understand this deep down in our hearts. When we come to encourage others, we must know it for ourselves. Encouragement from experience makes all the difference. When my wife and I went through our rough period, there were many who tried to encourage us, but so few who had that experience. No offense to the first group, but they had normal babies. Because of this, their words fell upon deaf ears, as in our hearts, we knew they didn't understand. Yet now when we talk to those who are going through what we did, we can encourage more for the sincerity and experience we have.

Our World Was Made For Trials

The critical point I've been working toward in this chapter is that the earth was created specifically as a place where mankind can be formed. God made the whole universe and we don't know what all is out there, but earth was made for us. On this earth is where the combination of sin, trials, and hardships can forge a spirit into this wondrous possibility of becoming like Christ. Our world is the furnace that can shape a son of God. I am not speaking of a child, but a son. This mix of trials can create those who can overcome and sit with Jesus. You don't really think God was surprised when Satan showed up and convinced Adam and Eve to eat the fruit, do you? Can you imagine God watching in the garden and going "oops, I didn't see that one coming"? God was after something; not just followers or children, but sons. God wanted those who could take up His name and move in His ways.

> For I consider that the sufferings of this present time
> are not worthy to be compared with the glory that is
> to be revealed to us. — (Romans 8:18)

Sufferings cannot compare to our reward. That is a good word to keep in your heart. These sufferings give us a chance to overcome and become approved. Imagine stepping before the God of all creation and hearing "well done." If you want to draw near to God, to become more like Jesus and be changed into His likeness, this is how it happens. As I slowly draw closer to the Lord I find that this is what I want more than anything. I want to be like Jesus. I want to be holy and set myself apart for the Lord. The more holy I am, the more of Him I can receive. As this desire gets stronger, the more I will take advantage of the hard times to pull closer to Him. They help make me like Jesus.

> But if you are without discipline, of which all have
> become partakers, then you are illegitimate children
> and not sons. — (Hebrews 12:8)

Trials aren't something we bring upon ourselves, our Father has laid them out before us. This should be a wake-up call for some of us. If you aren't being disciplined, then you aren't a child of God. I'm not saying that all trials are discipline. Many are tests, some are a result of sin in our lives, but there's also discipline from the Lord to keep us on track. Discipline to shape our growth and make us better. If you aren't feeling like things are coming your way to push and stretch you into being more like Christ, then you need to reassess where you are.

Consider It Joy

> Consider it all joy, my brethren, when you encounter
> various trials, knowing that the testing of your
> faith produces endurance. And let endurance have

> its perfect result, so that you may be perfect and complete, lacking in nothing. — (James 1:2–4)

Each time I read this verse, I just wonder at it. We can get so caught up in our lives that we forget what is important. I try to imagine if I could be "perfect and complete, lacking in nothing." How much would that please my Lord? How much could I be an encouragement and a help to those around me? How much could I be proud of what I've become? I long for such of thing. I dream that I could become more than I am, to become more like my beloved Jesus. It's taken me a while to understand this. I have understood the basic concept, but it's taken longer for it to hit home. I want to grow. That's the core of this chapter. I want a stronger faith and a better relationship with my Lord. I want to be like Jesus. To do this, I need to know Him better, but also to trust in Him. Unfortunately (or fortunately depending upon how you look at it) one of the quickest paths is through trials. This is part of why I haven't grown as much for a while. I wouldn't stand up under the trials. God has shown me a lot of things in the scriptures, but if I don't put them to use, then what use are they? As James said, "faith without works is dead." Over time, I have realized that the way I grow closest to God is to draw near to Him through my trials and difficulties. As I come to that conclusion, I begin to understand Paul's words.

> Therefore I will rejoice in weaknesses so that Christ's power may rest on me. That is why, for Christ's sake, I delight in weaknesses, in insults, in hardships, in persecutions, in difficulties. For when I am weak, then I am strong. — (2 Corinthians 12:9–10)

Now I find myself trying to "delight" in those times of difficulties. Can I say I look forward to them? No. Am I saying that I enjoy them at the time? Definitely not. What I'm saying is that I get to them and see the advantage of them much the same way as when I get tired while running. I know if I continue to push myself, I will grow stronger and get more endurance from pushing my body during times of pain. In the same way, during trials, if I'll put my trust in Jesus and continue to persevere under the trial, I will receive the reward. Peter tells us that after perseverance we find godliness. James tells us that it will make us "mature and complete." What I know is that it will draw me closer to my Lord.

Let me step off track for a quick second to make one admonition. Do not go asking for these trials. Let them come on their own. Jesus himself told us, "each day has enough trouble of its own" (Matthew 6:34). If you go looking for trials, you will find yourself stepping out of God's place for you. Worse, you might find yourself getting enjoyment from walking close to the edge of sin, which will lead you to falling more easily. Asking for temptations or trials may well be inviting the devil into your life. Instead, when they come, we should consider all of our obstacles, trials, and troubles as joy. That's tough, but it's a mindset. To know that this trial can make me more like Jesus and bring me closer to God gives me a hope and joy in it to stand firm through it.

Think of it as a shortcut to holiness. There are certain things that God will not give us before we've shown ourselves to be faithful with what He has already provided. It's like a parent with a child who has reached the legal driving age. If the child is responsible, the parents will let them drive the car, but if they've proven themselves irresponsible with what they already have, why would the parents hand them the keys? Similarly, trials are a chance to prove ourselves and to mature. Look at them for the opportunity that they are and use that joy to face them. Take joy from overcoming. Take advantage of what crosses your path, but don't go looking for it.

Joy Of The Lord

> The joy of the LORD is your strength — (Nehemiah 8:10)

I have wondered if this verse means the joy God has in us, or our joy that we have in God. Each time I get caught up in considering this, I come back to the same point: it works out to be the same. I say this since Jesus said He wanted our joy to be full, and for God's joy to fill us in John 15. God said when we keep His commandments, we will stay in His love; and He spoke this to us so that His joy may be in us. He finds joy in us following His commands. It's all intertwined.

No wonder the apostles could say to "consider it pure joy" when they face trials. We can find our joy in pleasing the Lord and becoming more like Him. The first part of that is that He finds joy in our obedience. Next, we're joyful in trials, because it makes us more like Jesus which also pleases Him. Think of it like motivation, what gives you the strength to do things like stay on a diet or go exercise? What's the reason that our new year's resolutions fall so quickly? Our motivation isn't based on something strong enough. But the joy of the Lord never fails. I finally came to realize something about where joy comes from. I had been equating joy with happiness, but it's not. If it were just happiness or having fun, then how could we find joy in a hardship? No, I finally realized that joy comes from a fulfilled purpose. I don't know if I heard this from someone, or the Lord just revealed it to me one day. How else could this verse about Jesus make any sense?

> For the joy set before him he endured the cross, scorning its shame, and sat down at the right hand of the throne of God. — (Hebrews 12:2)

Jesus knew the end result, and used the joy from fulfilling that work to take Himself to the cross.

Practice

> Therefore I urge you, brethren, by the mercies of God, to present your bodies a living and holy sacrifice, acceptable to God, which is your spiritual service of worship. — (Romans 12:1)

Make your bodies a living sacrifice. Remember this when you're up against a temptation. Most temptations are things that we want; something we're trying to keep ourselves from doing. In those cases, offer those feelings to the Lord as a sacrifice. Tell Him that He is more important and give Him this desire of yours as an act of love. Keep in mind what the sacrifice accomplishes. Don't resist temptation just to do it. If that's the case, you'll finally give in because it's not worth it. No, it's for the Lord. Use that as you're tempted, not allowing yourself to stray from His grace, for it is sufficient. If you try to do it under your own strength, sooner or later you will run out.

> Therefore if anyone is in Christ, he is a new creature; the old things passed away; behold, new things have come. — (2 Corinthians 5:17)

Think of it this way. You are no longer a sinner; you are no longer that old man. You have become a new creation. What does this mean? First, it means that the temptation is not from yourself. You could have old habits you want to do by routine; however, we know that God doesn't tempt us, so that leaves the enemy. There's a distinction there. If I'm fighting against myself, I seem to fail. A house divided against itself cannot stand. If one part of me wants something and the other part of me doesn't want it, I'm going to fail. But I'm new and my spirit's new, I have the mind of Christ. The temptation is not from me, it's from the devil, which means I'm already in the right place. I just need to stand my ground. Instead of fighting and fighting to do the right thing, I just tell the devil to go away. We spend so much time trying to change ourselves and fail because we believe that's just who we are. Trying to change is difficult. Once we realize God's already changed us, we just have to believe. Any attack is from the outside, it's someone else trying to force something on us, and that makes a fundamental difference that I can't put into words.

> But put on the Lord Jesus Christ, and make no provision for the flesh in regard to its lusts. — (Romans 13:14)

Each day (or many times a day), envision yourself changing clothes. Take that old man—with all the bad habits, sins, and such—and take him off. Then put on the new man that looks like Christ. I like to imagine this in my mind. I picture myself pulling off all these things from myself like a costume, and putting on an image of Christ. God has already remade you, and that person inside of you is waiting to come out. Choose the new man, put him on, and walk in him.

> Fixing our eyes on Jesus, the author and perfecter of faith, who for the joy set before Him endured the cross, despising the shame, and has sat down at the right hand of the throne of God. — (Hebrews 12:2)

Fix your eyes on Jesus. This doesn't just mean think about Him sometimes, or set Him as your example. This literally means to set your eyes upon Him. Look to Him (in your imagination of course), think on Him, and contemplate Him. Then, keep doing it. If you're looking to Jesus in everything you do, there's no time left to even ponder sin. You're too busy thinking about the King. The more you see Jesus, the more you change to be like Him. When temptation comes, with humility look at Jesus and be open. He is happy to help.

How do you know your progress? By the fruit of course. Galatians lists out the fruit of the spirit for us. Don't get it backward like many Christians do. They take a fruit like peace, realize it's not evident in their lives, and then they work on peace. Does a tree that's not producing apples go grab an apple and try to shove it onto its branches? No, that's just silly. We don't make the fruit of peace by trying to fix each action. This is not a process of fixing our actions but rather a process of walking under the spirit. The fruit is the result, not the path. This means if your life is lacking fruit, you're not walking right. Fix that. Ask the Lord to show you the path, focus upon Him, and spend your days pleasing Him. The fruit will follow. Notice that it is the fruit of the spirit, not fruits. It's not a set of things we do, but a single outgrowth of the Spirit within us.

Conclusion

> Beloved, I am not writing a new commandment to you, but an old commandment which you have had from the beginning; the old commandment is the word which you have heard. On the other hand, I am writing a new commandment to you, which is true in Him and in you, because the darkness is passing away and the true Light is already shining. — (1 John 1:8–9)

One of the great ironies of my faith is that after all these years of searching to draw near to God, I find the keys are still the same as when I began. The path to walking with Jesus is the same as it has always been: read the Word, pray, fast, and be humble. There were many challenges and obstacles to overcome, numerous truths I've found along the way, yet the path to intimacy is still upon my knees. It's our determination and perseverance which establish the level of relationship we can reach.

The building blocks are simple.

Humility – He's God. Let it permeate your every fiber. There's nothing of yours that is worthwhile apart from what He has for you.

Eat the Word – Read, meditate, and memorize. Feed upon it like your favorite dishes. Let it be always upon your lips. The very word of God is set before us, and it will transform us.

Pray – There is no compromise for time on your knees. I know some people are in situations where you can't get free. Those people know it, and God has an allowance for that, but most of us can make the time. Time in prayer will focus your spirit and open your heart. If you want to hear and see from the Lord, there is no shortcut. Be always in prayer. Live a life of prayer, making the most of each opportunity.

Waiting – This goes alongside prayer, that you should be ever listening. Don't clutter your mind, but keep it open to the Lord. Talk with Him, ask questions, but especially spend times just waiting for Him to speak. This clears your spiritual ears so that you can hear Him.

Sacrifice – Set aside things you desire and want, and put it toward God. Look to the Old Testament and you'll find that sacrifices invite God's presence. Turn off that show which doesn't glorify Him, set down your books, fast, and pray. Begin to set aside the things of your heart to find His. Take your thoughts and focus them upon the Lord.

I named this book the Jesus We Forgot, because so many of the revelations the Lord gave to me were things I already knew(or should have known), but had set aside. The steps toward the deeper path I found I knew, but didn't believe would work.

Draw near to God, for He can be found. In Him you will find all you need. It takes time, determination, and tears, but it's worth it. Don't continue in the old superficial Christian life but take the chance to live in Him.

Now go find Him.

About the Author

Brent Shores is a software developer who lives with his wife and daughter in Fayetteville, Arkansas. His desire is to show other Christians that the way to God is not just through their churches, but on their knees. He wishes to reveal the revelations the Lord has given him to come to know the Lord more deeply.